ARBITRARY BORDERS

Political Boundaries in World History

The Division of the Middle East
The Treaty of Sèvres

England and Northern Ireland
The Troubles

The Great Wall of China

The Green Line
The Division of Palestine

The Iron Curtain
The Cold War in Europe

The Mason–Dixon Line

Vietnam: The 17th Parallel

Korea Divided: The 38th Parallel and the Demilitarized Zone

The U.S.–Mexico Border
The Treaty of Guadalupe Hidalgo

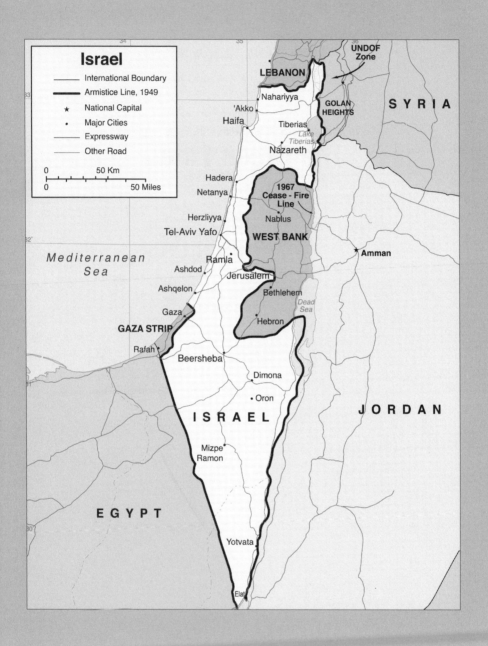

ARBITRARY BORDERS

Political Boundaries in World History

The Green Line
The Division of Palestine

Robert C. Cottrell

Foreword by
Senator George J. Mitchell

Introduction by
James I. Matray
California State University, Chico

CHELSEA HOUSE
PUBLISHERS
A Haights Cross Communications Company

Philadelphia

To My Daughter, Jordan Alexandra Cottrell

FRONTIS   Map of Israel shows the country's boundaries as defined by the 1949 Armistices.

CHELSEA HOUSE PUBLISHERS

VP, NEW PRODUCT DEVELOPMENT   Sally Cheney
DIRECTOR OF PRODUCTION   Kim Shinners
CREATIVE MANAGER   Takeshi Takahashi
MANUFACTURING MANAGER   Diann Grasse

Staff for THE GREEN LINE

EXECUTIVE EDITOR   Lee Marcott
PRODUCTION EDITOR   Noelle Nardone
PICTURE RESEARCH   21st Century Publishing Services
SERIES DESIGNER   Keith Trego
COVER DESIGNER   Keith Trego
LAYOUT   EJB Publishing Services

www.chelseahouse.com
A Haights Cross Communications Company

First Printing

9 8 7 6 5 4 3 2 1

Library of Congress Cataloging-in-Publication Data
Cottrell, Ro
The green l
p. cm. — (
Includes bi
ISBN 0-79
1. Arab-Isr
Boundaries—Juvenile literature. I. Title. II. Series.
DS119.7.C669 2004
956.05'3—dc22

2004006276

Contents

Foreword

Senator George J. Mitchell

I spent years working for peace in Northern Ireland and in the Middle East. I also made many visits to the Balkans during the long and violent conflict there.

Each of the three areas is unique; so is each conflict. But there are also some similarities: in each, there are differences over religion, national identity, and territory.

Deep religious differences that lead to murderous hostility are common in human history. Competing aspirations involving national identity are more recent occurrences, but often have been just as deadly.

Territorial disputes—two or more people claiming the same land—are as old as humankind. Almost without exception, such disputes have been a factor in recent conflicts. It is impossible to calculate the extent to which the demand for land—as opposed to religion, national identity, or other factors—figures in the motivation of people caught up in conflict. In my experience it is a substantial factor that has played a role in each of the three conflicts mentioned above.

In Northern Ireland and the Middle East, the location of the border was a major factor in igniting and sustaining the conflict. And it is memorialized in a dramatic and visible way: through the construction of large walls whose purpose is to physically separate the two communities.

In Belfast, the capital and largest city in Northern Ireland, the so-called "Peace Line" cuts through the heart of the city, right across urban streets. Up to thirty feet high in places, topped with barbed wire in others, it is an ugly reminder of the duration and intensity of the conflict.

In the Middle East, as I write these words, the government of Israel has embarked on a huge and controversial effort to construct a security fence roughly along the line that separates Israel from the West Bank.

Having served a tour of duty with the U.S. Army in Berlin, which was once the site of the best known of modern walls, I am skeptical of their long-term value, although they often serve short-term needs. But it cannot be said that such structures represent a new idea. Ancient China built the Great Wall to deter nomadic Mongol tribes from attacking its population.

In much the same way, other early societies established boundaries and fortified them militarily to achieve the goal of self-protection. Borders always have separated people. Indeed, that is their purpose.

This series of books examines the important and timely issue of the significance of arbitrary borders in history. Each volume focuses attention on a territorial division, but the analytical approach is more comprehensive. These studies describe arbitrary borders as places where people interact differently from the way they would if the boundary did not exist. This pattern is especially pronounced where there is no geographic reason for the boundary and no history recognizing its legitimacy. Even though many borders have been defined without legal precision, governments frequently have provided vigorous monitoring and military defense for them.

This series will show how the migration of people and exchange of goods almost always work to undermine the separation that borders seek to maintain. The continuing evolution of a European community provides a contemporary example illustrating this point, most obviously with the adoption of a single currency. Moreover, even former Soviet bloc nations have eliminated barriers to economic and political integration.

Globalization has emerged as one of the most powerful forces in international affairs during the twenty-first century. Not only have markets for the exchange of goods and services become genuinely worldwide, but instant communication and sharing of information have shattered old barriers separating people. Some scholars even argue that globalization has made the entire concept of a territorial nation-state irrelevant. Although the assertion is certainly premature and probably wrong, it highlights the importance of recognizing how borders often have reflected and affirmed the cultural, ethnic, or linguistic perimeters that define a people or a country.

Since the Cold War ended, competition over resources or a variety of interests threaten boundaries more than ever, resulting in contentious interaction, conflict, adaptation, and intermixture. How people define their borders is also a factor in determining how events develop in the surrounding region. This series will provide detailed descriptions of selected arbitrary borders in history with the objective of providing insights on how artificial boundaries separating people will influence international affairs during the next century.

Senator George J. Mitchell
October 2003

Introduction

James I. Matray
California State University, Chico

Throughout history, borders have separated people. Scholars have devoted considerable attention to assessing the significance and impact of territorial boundaries on the course of human history, explaining how they often have been sources of controversy and conflict. In the modern age, the rise of nation-states in Europe created the need for governments to negotiate treaties to confirm boundary lines that periodically changed as a consequence of wars and revolutions. European expansion in the nineteenth century imposed new borders on Africa and Asia. Many native peoples viewed these boundaries as arbitrary and, after independence, continued to contest their legitimacy. At the end of both world wars in the twentieth century, world leaders drew artificial and impermanent lines separating assorted people around the globe. Borders certainly are among the most important factors that have influenced the development of world affairs.

Chelsea House Publishers decided to publish a collection of books looking at arbitrary borders in history in response to the revival of the nuclear crisis in North Korea in October 2002. Recent tensions on the Korean peninsula are a direct consequence of Korea's partition at the 38th parallel at the end of World War II. Other nations in human history have suffered because of similar artificial divisions that have been the result of either international or domestic factors and often a combination of both. In the case of Korea, the United States and the Soviet Union decided in August 1945 to divide the country into two zones of military occupation ostensibly to facilitate the surrender of Japanese forces. However, a political contest was then underway inside Korea to determine the future of the nation after forty years of Japanese colonial rule. The Cold War then created two Koreas with sharply contrasting political, social, and economic systems that symbolized an ideological split among the Korean people. Borders separate people, but rarely prevent their economic, political, social, and cultural interaction. But in Korea, an artificial border has existed since 1945 as a nearly impenetrable barrier precluding meaningful contact between two portions of the same population. Ultimately, two authentic Koreas emerged, exposing how an arbitrary boundary can create circumstances resulting even in the permanent division of a homogeneous people in a historically united land.

Korea's experience in dealing with artificial division may well be unique, but it is not without historical parallels. The first set of books in this series on arbitrary boundaries will provide description and analysis of the division of the Middle East after World War I, the Iron Curtain in Central Europe during the Cold War, the United States-Mexico border, the 17th parallel in Vietnam, and the Mason-Dixon Line. A second set of books will address the Great Wall in China, the Green Line in Israel, and the 38th parallel and demilitarized zone in Korea. Finally, there will be volumes describing how discord over artificial borders in the Louisiana Territory, Northern Ireland, and Czechoslovakia reflected fundamental disputes about sovereignty, religion, and ethnicity. Admittedly, there are many significant differences between these boundaries, but these books will strive to cover as many common themes as possible. In so doing, each will help readers conceptualize how complex factors such as colonialism, culture, and economics determine the nature of contact between people along these borders. Although globalization has emerged as a powerful force working against the creation and maintenance of lines separating people, boundaries likely will endure as factors having a persistent influence on world events. This series of books will provide insights about the impact of arbitrary borders on human history and how such borders continue to shape the modern world.

James I. Matray
Chico, California
April 2004

1

The Setting
of Armistice Lines

With fighting still raging in the Middle East, Israeli and Arab delegates met on the picturesque Greek island of Rhodes, situated a dozen miles southwest of Turkey, beginning on January 13, 1949. In shaping a series of armistices over the course of the next few months, those representatives created the framework for arbitrary borders that divided Palestine between the Jewish state of Israel and its Arab neighbors. That territorial partition came to be known as the Green Line, although analysts dispute whether it involved Egypt and the Gaza Strip in addition to Israel, Jordan, and the West Bank. Shifting slivers of land in the north also formed a demilitarized zone separating Israel and Syria, as required by another agreement established in Hirbet Warda (located between Mahanayim and Mishmar Hayarden). Not participating in the discussions, and little mentioned as they unfolded, were spokesmen for Palestinian refugees, who had fled their homes when war intensified in the Middle East during the previous springtime. The Israeli and Arab negotiators—other than the Syrians, who appeared willing to take on 300,000 refugees—shared a lack of concern for the Palestinians but had little else in common other than a desire to end the fighting. Israeli Prime Minister David Ben-Gurion rejected the offer by Syrian leader Colonel Husni Zaim to accept Palestinian refugees.

The Green Line boundaries, or armistice lines, came to be viewed by the world community and by the combatants themselves, albeit to a lesser extent, as "de facto international frontiers," historian Bennie Morris contends.[1] The selected borders were not part of actual peace treaties, however, and did not result in diplomatic and commercial dealings between the formerly warring parties. In the period ahead, the Arab states graphically demonstrated that they considered the armistices to be only temporary, allowing for at most a momentary cessation of hostilities. The Israelis, including Prime Minister Ben-Gurion, saw the agreements in a different light, with some likening them to "de facto peace agreements" that purportedly diminished the need to carve out formal peace treaties, although others believed that such agreements still had to be produced.[2]

Like the war itself, the stark differences characterizing Israeli and Arab negotiators underscored how difficult it would be to establish a Jewish state with clearly defined borders within the boundaries of Palestine. Establishing such territorial borders would necessarily be both arbitrary and unsettling for many longtime inhabitants as well as for more recent immigrants to the region, no matter what historical and religious forces had led them there. The problems that Israeli and Arab representatives in Rhodes encountered in resolving their differences only foreshadowed decades of trauma and war; this in turn highlighted the tenuous nature of efforts to carve out arbitrary borders in the Middle East. The volatile mix of Jews, Arabs, and Christians, with European, North African, Middle Eastern, and North American roots, ensured that this endeavor would prove trying indeed.

It was both ironic and fitting that many of the most crucial negotiations in the setting of artificial boundaries took place on the island of Rhodes, with its breathtaking coastline, fertile valleys, and generally mild climate. Earlier an independent state, Rhodes had come under the sway of an array of potent city-states or empires, from Athens to Rome. A way station for Christian crusaders, Rhodes, whose Colossus was one of the Seven Wonders of the Ancient World, was occupied by the Knights Hospitallers of Saint John in 1310 before being conquered by the Ottoman Turks in 1522. The Turko-Italian War of 1911–1912 resulted in a change of possession, which did not end until after World War II.

Fascist occupation of Rhodes began in late 1936 and terminated the tranquil conditions generally experienced by both Jews and Muslims on the island. Each group admittedly experienced intolerance at various points. Jews suffered legal disabilities, were required to wear distinctive yellow badges, and were accused of blood libel—the contention that Jews murdered Christians to use their blood during Passover services. Muslims endured prejudicial treatment themselves, along with violence and repression. Both groups suffered economic and political traumas during the first part of the nineteenth century, which undoubtedly convinced some elderly Jews to immigrate to Palestine. In the initial stages of the twentieth century, a growing number of Jews from Rhodes, many influenced by liberal or socialist ideals, opted to make *aliyah* (emigration) to Palestine or at least to study Hebrew there. More wanted to leave once fascism enveloped the island. Conditions worsened in July 1944 after German forces took control of Rhodes. Over 1700 Jews were transported to Germany in German boats, with nearly 1600 eventually dying at Auschwitz or in other concentration camps. By the time the British occupation began, a mere 50 Jews remained on the island.

In early 1949, Rhodes again became a location where the interests of Jews and Muslims coincided. On November 29, 1947, the United Nations had devised Resolution 181, which called for the partitioning of Palestine into a Jewish state that controlled more than half the land, although Jews composed only one-third of the population. Reluctantly, Jewish leaders, led by Ben-Gurion, agreed to the plan, but Arab governments opposed it. After Ben-Gurion proclaimed the establishment of the state of Israel on May 14, 1948, nearby Arab nations—Lebanon, Syria, Jordan, Egypt, and Iraq—attacked the new Jewish nation. When the war ended, Israel controlled an additional 77 percent of land with its expanded borders inside the Green Line; Egypt and Jordan held the other 23 percent of territory that was to have made up a Palestinian state. Hundreds of thousands of Palestinians had fled from their homes to begin a diaspora some likened to that of the Jews, whose own wanderings were the impetus for the creation of the state of Israel.

On November 29, 1948, one year to the day after the United Nations passed ill-fated Resolution 181, Jordanian diplomat Abdulla el-Tel suggested that Jordan and Israel conduct a diplomatic swap. Jordan wanted an armistice that would rely on UN Resolution 181, whereas Israel sought to benefit territorially from its military successes by establishing new artificial borders. Both sides had apparently agreed, albeit informally, to divide territory in general along with control of Jerusalem; they also had evidently decided to exclude the Palestinians from determining their own fate. El-Tel called for Israel to control the Jewish Quarter in the Old City, and for Jordan to govern the Arab Katamon Quarter. The Latrun road, situated midway between Jerusalem and Tel Aviv, was to be opened to traffic from both sides. Reluctant to give up the Katamon Quarter, Ben-Gurion declined the offer. One week later, el-Tel suggested that Jordan would consider relinquishing a portion of Latrun and would allow for joint, regional Arab-Jewish security forces. King Abdullah called for various Arab refugees to return to Lod and Ramla, however. Jordan accepted Israeli Colonel Moshe Dayan's proposal for a reopening of the railway line between Tel Aviv and Jerusalem, although that required movement through a small amount of Arab land. For its part, Jordan hoped to be allowed to make use of the road from Bethlehem up to the Jaffa Gate in Jerusalem. Ben-Gurion again quashed the attempted compromise.

Nevertheless, Ben-Gurion insisted in mid-December, "Our primary aim now is peace," declaring, "Our future need is peace and friendship with the Arabs."[3] On December 29, 1948, el-Tel seemed to suggest to Dayan that King Abdullah also desired a general peace settlement. Indeed, el-Tel urged talks to begin immediately in Jerusalem and, if necessary, to be conducted alternately in Jordanian and Israeli buildings. The discussions opened the following evening at 6:30 P.M. in the Jordanian sector, with Dayan and Reuven Shiloah of the foreign ministry representing Israel. Ben-Gurion ordered Dayan and Shiloah to persist with the negotiations, even if those sessions did not go well initially, but the battle with Egyptians forces continued to take place in the Negev. The Israeli prime minister also indicated that nothing definitive should be determined regarding Jordanian control of the West Bank. Similarly, he stated that no firm decision should be made about the southernmost border of Israel alongside Jordan. On the other hand, the Israeli negotiators were permitted to discuss the possibility of granting Jordanian access in Gaza. They were to challenge Jordanian control over Ramla and Jaffa, however, although not dismissing outright Jordan's dominion in Lod.

During a series of meetings on the island of Rhodes in early 1949, Arab and Israeli delegates created a system of borders that divided Palestine between Israel and the surrounding Arab nations. Here, United Nations mediators and representatives from Egypt and Israel gather to sign the armistice between the two countries on March 1, 1949.

In the meantime, the Israeli army under Yigal Allon penned in their Egyptian counterparts along the Mediterranean coast. Armistice talks were initiated at the aged but elegant Hotel des Roses on the island of Rhodes. To Allon's dismay, Ben-Gurion refused to allow him to crush the Egyptian forces altogether or to take control of the West Bank. An embittered Allon sent Lieutenant Colonel Yitzhak Rabin to serve as the Israeli representative from the southern front at the conference in Rhodes. Rabin was greatly impressed with the leadership afforded by Dr. Ralph Bunche, who had replaced Count Folke Bernadotte as the United Nation's chief mediator on Palestine. Bernadotte had recently been assassinated by members of the *Lohamei Herut Israel*, or Stern gang, a Jewish terrorist group. A deadlock ensued after the Egyptians demanded that the Israeli Defense Force (IDF) renounce the large territorial gains attained in the Negev since mid-October. The Egyptians also wanted Israel to with-draw from Beersheba; the Israelis insisted that Egypt abandon claim to the Gaza Strip. After considerable haggling, the Egyptians agreed on February 24, 1949, to accept the recognized international boundary separating their state and Israel, with Egyptian forces regaining control of Gaza. Seven Israeli outposts along the Gaza Strip were retained. With the completion of the Israeli-Egyptian armistice and the expansion of Israel's artificial boundaries, Ben-Gurion enthusiastically commented, "After the creation of the state and our victories in battle—this is the great event of a great and marvelous year."[4]

Negotiations between Israel and Jordan were lengthier and more complicated. The first session in late December 1948 had accomplished little, but the second gathering proved more fruit-ful. That meeting occurred on the evening of January 5, 1949, at a site near the Mandelbaum Gate and verified that marked dif-ferences characterized the two parties. King Abdullah wanted there to be a corridor through the Negev that would connect Jordan and Egypt and demanded all of Jerusalem, other than the Jewish Quarter. In addition, Abdullah continued to insist that Jordan take over the Katamon Quarter and other sections of the New City. Finally, he called for Kibbutz Ramat Rahel, located just outside Jerusalem, to be held by Jordan. Through el-Tel, Abdullah expressed a willingness for the suburbs of Lift and Romena, already in Israeli hands, to come under the control of the Jewish state. After being informed about the conditions set by the Jordanians, Ben-Gurion called for the talks to continue. "We must probe every possibility of achieving peace. We need it probably more than the Jordanians—though no doubt they are losing more than a little, becoming more and more subservient to the British."[5]

Following Ben-Gurion's lead, Dayan arranged another meet-ing with el-Tel, which was scheduled for the same location on January 14. At the same time, Dayan informed el-Tel that war would eventuate if Jordan did not prove more conciliatory. El-Tel also worried about the futility of continuing talks near the Mandelbaum Gate. Consequently, he relayed Abdullah's offer to meet at the Shuneh palace in Amman. A pair of meetings with the Jordanian king ensued, one on January 16 and the other two weeks later. In the first session, Dayan and Elias Sasson of the Israeli Foreign Ministry met with el-Tel and Abdullah; at the second meeting, Taufiq Abu al-Huda, the king's prime minister, was also present. The king soon declared that his nation, in the fashion of the other Arab states that had warred with Israel, would sign an armistice agreement with Israel. For his part, Abdullah indicated his readiness to move beyond an armistice to explore a peace treaty between Jordan and Israel. Such an undertaking, Abdullah stated, should occur in public and take place without United Nations' involvement.

Abdullah, who was closely following Israel's dealings with Egypt, warned that Gaza should not be ceded to the powerful Arab state. Jordan, Abdullah pointed out, required access through Gaza to the Mediterranean Sea. Indeed, Abdullah went so far as to declare, "Take it yourselves, give it to the devil, but don't let Egypt have it!"[6] Dayan came to respect Abdullah, who appeared to be "a wise man and a leader who could make critical decisions."[7] More formal negotiations between Jordan and Israel occurred on the island of Rhodes, beginning at 4:30 P.M. on March 1, 1949, only days after the accord had been signed between Israel and Egypt. Reuven Shiloah led the Israeli negotiating team, with Dayan serving as his deputy, while Colonel Ahmed Sudki el-Jundi guided the Jordanian delegation.

The proceedings unfolded in the yellow room of the Hotel des Roses, with Dr. Bunche again serving as chief mediator. The first session opened with something of a crisis. Bunche had convinced the two parties to greet one another formally on entering the council chamber. After arriving at the meeting site, however, the Israeli representatives discovered that the Jordanians were already seated. Bunche immediately requested that Colonel Jundi rise so that a formal introduction to Shiloah could take place. On witnessing Jundi decline Bunche's suggestion, a stunned Shiloah was visibly taken aback. As matters turned out, the Jordanians did not realize that they had violated any codes of etiquette, and Jundi eventually apologized for the misunderstanding.

Fortunately, relations warmed up after the first session, and a number of informal meetings took place. Nevertheless, no progress occurred over the course of the first 10 days. As Dayan remembered, the location of the negotiations was a saving grace:

> All the rest was most pleasant—good food, spring weather, enchanting scenery, and interesting company. I spent much of my free time walking along the beach, inspecting the old Turkish fort, and wandering in the woods. Hundreds of butterflies of all sizes and colors flitted between the bushes, giving a fairy-tale air to the site.[8]

Greatly aiding matters was the deft stewardship of Dr. Bunche, who helped establish a receptive atmosphere and diligently strove to keep the negotiations on track. Notwithstanding Bunche's painstaking efforts, there was one particular sticking point: access to holy shrines. Bunche also had to contend with the ongoing hostilities between Israeli and Jordanian military units; the Jordanians had witnessed Israel take control of the southern Negev down to the Gulf of Aqaba, something Jordan had hoped to avoid. A cease-fire agreement became effective on March 11. Dayan was ordered to return to Jerusalem, where he and a group of Israeli delegates again met with el-Tel, King Abdullah, and other Jordanian representatives. In the early morning hours of March 23 (the very day an armistice was reached with Lebanon, with recognition of the old Lebanon-Palestine border), an agreement was reached, on the heels of threats by Israel to grab parts of Samaria. Abdullah had worried that the entire West Bank might fall under Israeli occupation. Thus, he had unsuccessfully sought to persuade both Great Britain and the United States to guarantee existing borders would be considered territorial frontiers or to ensure Jordanian hegemony (dominance) on the West Bank. Later in the day, Abdullah proclaimed that peace had been attained.

On April 3, the Israel–Trans-Jordan Armistice was inked on the island of Rhodes. Bunche delivered the following proclamation to the signatories, the Israelis Shiloah and Dayan and the Jordanians Jundi and Colonel Mouaita: "You have ensured the return of peace to Palestine. You have used pens, not swords. You have applied reason, not force, and you have reached agreement."[9] Noting that the armistice ensured the abatement of hostilities between two of the most significant parties in the Middle Eastern conflict, Bunche declared, "It covers a combined front which extends over the greater part of Palestine. It commits Trans-Jordan and Israel to a virtual non-aggression pact. It sets up machinery whereby the two parties can, and I am sure will, continue to work out their differences amicably and constructively and by direct consultations."[10] Bunche then stated that the agreement offered the promise of addressing the issue of Palestinian refugees, whom he deemed "by and large ... the innocent victims of the dispute."[11]

The actual terms of the armistice included injunctions against both employing military force to resolve the question of Palestine and resorting to aggressive action; the armistice also ensuring the right of both Jordan and Israel to be secure against possible attack by the other party. Regarding the armistice demarcation lines, the agreement prohibited "civilians from crossing the fighting lines or entering the area between the lines."[12] In Jerusalem, those lines, which established the equivalent of arbitrary borders in the Holy City, were supposed to "correspond to the lines defined in the 30 November 1948 Cease-Fire Agreement."[13] A special committee, composed of two Israelis and two Jordanians and selected by their respective governments, was to help ensure compliance with various parts of the Armistice. These included the following:

> resumption of the normal functioning of the cultural and humanitarian institutions on Mount Scopus and free access thereto; free access to the Holy Places and cultural institutions and use of the cemetery on the Mount of Olives; resumption of the Latrun pumping station; provision of electricity for the Old City; and resumption of operation of the railroad to Jerusalem.[14]

Significantly, however, as the *United Nations Bulletin* of April

15, 1949, related, the Israel–Trans-Jordan Armistice established demarcation lines "without prejudice to any territorial settlements of boundaries."[15] Jordan ceded a strip of territory, from three to five miles wide, that swept southwest of Qalqilya in a line northward to Wadi 'Ara; the strip continued to a spot just outside the northern sector of Jenin. This land contained approximately 15 Arab villages and some 20,000 inhabitants. In return, Israel handed over a smaller stretch of land, located to the southeast of Dhahiriya. The final armstice agreement was signed with Syria on July 20, in which the international boundary was accepted and demilitarized zones, including land situated on the eastern side of the Sea of Galilee, were established.

The armistices and the arbitrary borders (or Green Line) that they shaped ensured that Israel was now in possession of greater territory than had been foreseen by the United Nations. Many problems remained, however, as historian-journalist Tom Segev notes. The border containing the Gaza Strip remained porous and susceptible to terrorist traffic. The partition line dividing Israel from Jordan was, in Segev's words, "entirely arbitrary, often in total disregard of the disrupted population on the spot." As a consequence of the decisions made in Rhodes, Jerusalem, and Amman, "thousands of Arab villagers found themselves living on the Israeli side of the line, while some of their lands remained on the Jordanian side."[16] At the same time, certain Arab territory, although still officially under the Jordanian flag, was now watched over by Israel. Infiltrators could readily violate the border separating these two countries, as they could the one to the west, while Jewish settlements located along the border were precariously exposed. Jerusalem itself was splintered with new artificial divisions and came to feature barbed-wire fences along with minefields. Despite the Israeli–Trans-Jordan Armistice, gunfire soon rang out across the demarcation line. As matters turned out, access to Mount Scopus, Hebrew University, the Hadassah Hospital, the Mount of Olives, and the Western, or Wailing, Wall remained highly limited.

2

The Shifting
Borders
of Palestine

The armistice agreements—devised in Rhodes, close by Rosh Hanikrah, and near Mishmar Hayarden—considerably expanded the arbitrary boundaries proposed for a Jewish state approximately 20 months earlier; at the same time, those agreements seemingly ended the possibility of establishing a Palestinian state. Those developments only continued the historic tradition of shifting the borders of Palestine once again. Both Judaism and Christianity emerged in the desert lands of Palestine, and the followers of Islam also considered this territory sacred. Before any of those great religions had emerged, however, the land itself was called Canaan, named after a Semitic people with roots from Mesopotamia and ancient Syria who dominated this area for approximately 1,500 years beginning about 3000 B.C. The Canaanites produced a linear alphabet, from which Hebrew was derived.

Early in the reign of the Canaanites, the Hebrews (or Israelites), who had departed from Mesopotamia, appeared in Canaan. Over the next several centuries, many Hebrews migrated to Egypt. While there, Hebrews may well have been exposed to monotheism (belief in one god), which the Pharaoh Akhenaton had introduced, although many Egyptians remained polytheistic (believing in multiple gods). During the 1200s B.C., Moses, who had been raised in the household of the pharaoh, led the Hebrews on an exodus out of Egypt to Canaan. There, the Hebrews, who believed that God had chosen them to rule over Canaan, battled other peoples, including the Philistines. Around 1000 B.C., newly selected King David united the 12 Hebrew tribes into the Kingdom of Israel, which had its own artificial boundaries with its capital located in reconstructed Jerusalem. David's son and successor Solomon ordered the First Temple to be constructed, as a tribute to God. After Solomon's death in 922 B.C., the northern and southern tribes splintered into Israel and Judah, respectively; the inhabitants of Judah came to be referred to as Jews, as did all Hebrews.

In the ninth century B.C., Israel and Judah together possessed territory that swept to the Mediterranean Sea and ran from the

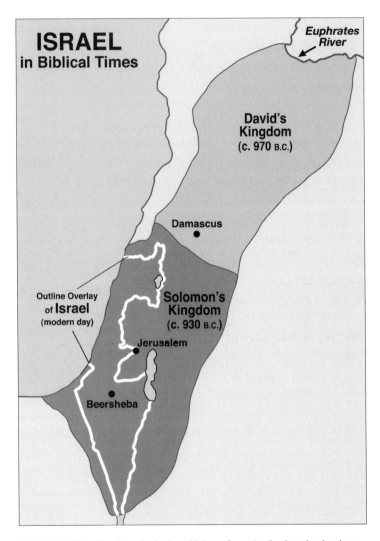

ISRAEL
in Biblical Times

Euphrates
River

David's
Kingdom
(c. 970 B.C.)

Damascus

Outline Overlay
of Israel
(modern day)

Solomon's
Kingdom
(c. 930 B.C.)

Jerusalem

Beersheba

The lands of Palestine have had a long history of constantly changing borders and inhabitants. This map shows the region and its boundaries during biblical times.

Golan Heights in the north (where present-day Syria exists) to Gaza and the Sinai Peninsula in the south. It followed along the coast and then from the northern edge of the Gulf of Aqaba to the eastern side of the Dead Sea and Lake Tiberias. As historian Charles D. Smith notes, these borders "were not static."[17] The Jews frequently took control of territory situated to the east of the Jordan River and briefly held land north of Damascus, along with the Golan Heights. At other points, the Jews were restricted to the territory claimed by Judah.

In about 722 B.C., the Assyrians took control of Israel. In 586 B.C., the Babylonians, who had supplanted the Assyrians in Mesopotamia, drove many Jews into exile, although some remained in Jerusalem. A half-century later, the Persian king Cyrus took over Palestine and soon permitted a group of Jews to resettle in Jerusalem, where they helped rebuild the temple. The Greeks, under Alexander the Great, subdued the Persian Empire around 331 B.C. By 200 B.C., the Syrian-based Seleucids held sway in Jerusalem, eventually prohibiting the practice of Judaism. This resulted in a revolt spearheaded by the Maccabees, who pushed the Seleucids out of Palestine by 140 B.C. Religiously inspired and encouraged by the Romans, the Maccabees subjugated northern portions of Samaria and the Galilee.

The Maccabees established an independent state, Judah, which the Romans conquered in 63 B.C. and renamed Judea. The Romans granted the Jews considerable political and religious freedom provided that they acknowledged Roman control. King Herod the Great rebuilt the Temple and attained control over large portions of southern Syria but displeased many of his fellow Jews, including the Zealots, who condemned Roman rule. In A.D. 66, the Zealots initiated a fierce battle against the Romans that ended with the burning of Jerusalem, the destruction of the Temple, and the capture of the stronghold at Masada, which culminated with the mass suicide of its defenders. The Bar Kokhba revolt, supported by Rabbi Akiva, began in A.D. 132, leading to the ouster of Jews from Jerusalem, the destruction of scores of Jewish fortresses, the razing of nearly 1,000 settlements, and the killing of more than 500,000 Jews. Because Galilee had not joined in the revolt, Jews there were permitted to continue practicing their religion. Indeed, the region became the new focal point of Jewish life; the *Mishna*, which codified Jewish law, was produced there around A.D. 200. Overall, however, the Bar Kokhba rebellion decimated the Jewish population of Judea, with thousands of survivors forced into slavery, many women compelled to resort to prostitution, and Jews forbidden to enter Jerusalem. Still, the Romans generally lightened their grip on Palestine once the revolt was suppressed, allowing Jews to practice their religion provided that they made no effort to convert Gentiles.

As the practitioners of Judaism endured trying times in Palestine, those of a new religion, birthed from Judaism, did also. Jesus Christ, a Jewish religious leader with particular appeal to the poor and outcasts—who viewed him as the long-awaited Messiah—dwelled in Palestine until being crucified by the Romans around A.D. 30. His followers, who were also Palestinian Jews, argued that Jesus was resurrected before ascending to heaven. A religious Jew, Paul of Tarsus, helped spread the gospel of the new sect, which was called Christianity. Paul offended orthodox Jews, contending that Jesus was the son of God, not merely a distant relative of King David. Shortly after a series of missionary endeavors by Paul, the Roman Emperor Nero began to persecute Christians, charging them with having burned Rome. In the first full century of the Common Era (the period dating from the birth of Jesus), the final gospels of the New Testament were composed.

Roman emperors generally adopted a tolerant attitude toward Christians, although pogroms and harassment were not uncommon during the second century. In 312, the Emperor Constantine insisted that Christians be afforded tolerance and eventually proclaimed himself a Christian. Because Jesus had acquired his first followers in Palestine, this region was viewed as a sacred place by Christians. The adoption of Christianity as an official state religion in the eastern Roman Empire resulted in efforts to restrict the religious practices of Jews, who suffered from discriminatory legislation.

The reign of Justinian (527–562) saw both the institution of additional restrictive measures prohibiting the construction of synagogues and mob action directed against Jews. In 614, the Sassanid Dynasty of Persia briefly took control of Palestine, although Byzantine rule soon returned to the region.

As matters turned out, the Christian restoration proved short lived. In 634, Arabs attacked Gaza, and four years later they moved into Jerusalem. The vast bulk of these Semitic people had long been nomadic shepherds, who eventually resided in the Near East. By the time they invaded Palestine, many Arabs were drawn to the teachings of Muhammad (570–632), who was viewed as the prophet of Allah. Muhammad's words would be written down in the *Koran*, which provided the foundation for the *sharia*, or Islamic law; thus, Muslims, like Jews and Christians, are considered "a people of a Book," as historian J. M. Roberts writes.[18] Beginning almost immediately after Muhammad's death, Arab armies—called Saracens by the Byzantines—conquered vast expanses of land, including large portions of Syria, Palestine, and Egypt, by 640. For the next 90 years, the reach of Islam, a monotheistic religion, widened into Europe and India as well as across Central Asia. Muslims, torn about who was the legitimate heir to Muhammad, splintered into two major factions: the Sunni and the Shi'i.

For many years, Palestine occupied a relatively minor role in the life of Muslims, although Jerusalem was considered a sacred site because of its important role in Judeo-Christian practice. Only Mecca, the birthplace of Muhammad, and Medina, where Muhammad began to acquire greater support from other Arabs, were considered holier locations by Muslims. From 661 to 750, the Umayyad Dynasty, which was Sunni and based in Damascus, governed Jerusalem and built the Dome of the Rock. Attention to the region lessened when the Abbasids, who were also Sunni but resided in Baghdad, established their hold over Jerusalem. In the last part of the ninth century, Ahmad ibn Tulun, a Sunni Muslim who ruled Egypt, controlled Palestine; another Egyptian dynasty, the Fatimids, who were Shi'i, were the overlords from 969 until the end of the eleventh century, when Christian crusaders captured Jerusalem.

During the early Muslim rule, Palestine remained a holy place for Jews, Christians, and Muslims, many of whom conducted a pilgrimage there. For the most part, Muslim governors allowed

Jerusalem is at the center of the Holy Lands for three of the world's major religions: Islam, Judaism, and Christianity. This overview of Jerusalem shows two sacred religious landmarks: the Dome of the Rock to the left and the Wailing Wall in the foreground.

both Jews and Christians to practice their faiths and to construct synagogues or churches; Muslims viewed the nonbelievers as *dhimmis*, who received protection so long as they submitted to Muslim governance. Important Jewish communities existed in Jerusalem, as well as in Banias, Tyre, Acre, Haifa, Ashkelon, Gaza, Tiberias, and Ramleh. The era of tolerance ended, however, with the Crusades, which resulted in tremendous bloodletting and a determination to convert Jerusalem into a Christian city that allowed no Muslim or Jewish cults or non-Christian residents. Notwithstanding the edicts regarding Jerusalem, the badly outnumbered Crusaders were forced to treat non-Christians fairly tolerantly. Jewish communities continued to thrive, particularly in coastal areas.

Christian dominance ended in 1187, when the Muslim ruler Saladin recaptured the city. In Europe, a drive to settle in Israel resulted in " 'the aliyah [immigration] of the three hundred rabbis' from France and England."[19] A dynastic struggle, as additional

Crusades were conducted, led to a brief period of Christian pre-eminence from 1229 to 1244. Shortly thereafter, Egyptian and Syrian-based Mameluke rulers, composed of military elites, established an empire that soon included Palestine. The Mamelukes strove to ensure that Jerusalem stood as a holy shrine for Muslims, Jews, and Christians alike. Although the Jewish settlement in Acre fell by the wayside, other communities continued in Safed, Gaza, Hebron, the Upper Galilee, and Jerusalem. Spurred by anti-Jewish violence and expulsions, Ashkenazi Jews from eastern or central Europe, Sephardi from Spain, and Jews from the Far East congregated in the great Holy City.

The dissipation of Mameluke authority helped set the stage for the Ottoman Turks to become, by 1517, the new overlords of Palestine, a position they held for four full centuries. The bulk of the Palestinian populace was made up of Arab Muslims, although Jews from across the region migrated to Jerusalem and other sections of Palestine throughout the period of Ottoman rule. The governor in Damascus ruled over Jerusalem, sometimes saddling its inhabitants with onerous taxes. Nevertheless, pluralism characterized Ottoman society, with mob action against Jews or Christians discouraged. Jews involved in mercantile pursuits, in particular, experienced various opportunities during the first two centuries of Ottoman rule. Conditions changed in the eighteenth century, however, owing to efforts by European states to strengthen Christian communities in the Ottoman Empire. Both Russian pilgrims and Greek Orthodox clergy, for example, were afforded increasingly greater access to Palestine. Thanks to preferential treatment, European merchants and middlemen came to dominate more of the regional trade and commerce.

By the latter stages of the nineteenth century, Palestine had experienced a series of dramatic regime and territorial changes that resulted in arbitrary borders of various casts. Some of these involved claims regarding the physical landscape, but others pertained to religious and cultural forces, which could themselves be liberating or restrictive. Palestine represented a blessed place for three of the world's great religions: Judaism, Christianity, and Islam. At different times, followers of those religions had coexisted, sometimes more easily than at other points, but there had also been efforts to compel "nonbelievers" to accept one true faith or to abandon the Holy Land altogether. As a new century approached, Palestine again became a focal point for religious and cultural clashes, with imperial actors vying for control of the land itself, which had already experienced many territorial shifts and alterations. In the process, it became clear that Palestine would have difficulty in accommodating the assortment of different peoples, who possessed markedly different hopes and aspirations.

3

The Unbounded Jewish Diaspora and a Return to Palestine

As the physical and territorial borders of Palestine underwent arbitrary alterations, so, too, did the composition of its inhabitants. Thus, throughout its long history, Palestine experienced demographic boundaries that sometimes restricted Jews, Christians, or Muslims from residing there. On other occasions, authorities welcomed one or all of those groups, while adhering to the belief that Jerusalem was a sacred site. Beginning in the nineteenth century, Jews, compelled by both religious and secular considerations, began to migrate to Palestine, notwithstanding opposition from Turkish authorities, who worried about the presence of another "national" problem within the empire. Concerns about an increase in anti-Semitism and actual pogroms also drove Jews to look to the ancient Holy Land as a possible refuge for their religious kin.

For a period beginning with the French Revolution at the end of the eighteenth century, worries regarding anti-Semitism appeared to be subsiding. The French Declaration of the Rights of Man and of the Citizen seemingly promised civil emancipation for all, including Jews, provided that they relinquished their group identity. Equality under the law was a guiding principle for the new and transformed states that emerged in Western Europe during the nineteenth century and was eagerly accepted by many Jews, who were associated with the *Haskalah* (enlightenment) movement, which favored Jewish integration into existing societies. At the same time, anti-Semitic feelings had never dissipated entirely and soon gained new adherents, especially in Eastern Europe in the last three decades of the century.

Many took offense at the increased visibility of Jews in urban areas and the social mobility experienced by Jews in professional positions, commerce, journalism, the arts, and left-wing political movements as they broke through arbitrary restrictions of all casts. Older stereotypes, which had emerged under medieval Christianity about the diabolical nature of Jews, resurfaced in a new fashion. Now, tales abounded of Jews conspiring to control economic and political developments worldwide. A new, virulent anti-Semitism, rooted in racist ideas, propounded easy solutions to what was known as the "Jewish question." Anti-Semitic publications proliferated, and pogroms abounded in Russia, spurred by the assassination of Tzar Alexander II in March 1881. His successor, Alexander III, targeted Jews in an effort to divert attention from the vast problems that afflicted the Russian people.

Responding immediately to the outbreak of violence, Eastern European Jews increasingly chose to emigrate, with the vast majority heading to the United States. A small but growing number opted for Palestine, where some 24,000 Jews resided. As early as 1862, the German radical Moses Hess published *Rome and Jerusalem*, which called for a return of Jews to Palestine, where brotherhood—absent class or racial strife—would purportedly prevail. The flood of pogroms (massacres) in Russia led many Haskalah supporters, including the *Chovevei Zion* (lovers of Zion), to become ardent champions of Jewish colonization of Palestine. Zionists believed that Jews must emancipate themselves; they required a territory with necessarily artificial borders where they could establish a secular state and where Jewish culture and the Hebrew language could be revitalized. The Russian Eliezer Ben-Yehuda, one of those who immigrated to Palestine in 1881, led the campaign to revive the language of Hebrew, which appeared to be withering away.

A few hundred members of the Chovevei Zion chose to immigrate to Palestine, as did even more who were involved in another group, BILU (*Beit Ya'akov Lekhu ve-Nelkhah*). The BILU students foresaw the creation of a Jewish nation in Palestine, based on Jewish agriculture and labor. Altogether, some 20,000 to 30,000 Jews went to Palestine during the first aliyah in this era, although fewer than 3,000 ended up in newly constructed cooperative agrarian villages, the *moshavot*. Those enterprises received financial support largely from wealthy Jews in Western Europe, especially Baron Edmond de Rothschild, who provided 1.6 million pounds sterling during the 1880s.

The Zionist movement soon acquired the leader it sorely needed: an Austrian lawyer and journalist, Theodore Herzl. Knowing little about Palestine or Zionism, Herzl tracked the

anti-Semitism that resulted in the public humiliation and pros-
ecution of Alfred Dreyfus, a Jewish captain in the French army,
who was wrongly accused of betraying his country. In early
1896, Herzl, then an ardent Zionist, predicted in *Der Judenstaat*
(*The Jewish State*), "The Jews who wish for a state will have it."[20]
Herzl helped establish the World Zionist Organization, which
called for the establishment of a Jewish homeland in Palestine.
After unsuccessfully seeking to garner support from the
Ottoman Empire, Herzl heard British colonial secretary, Joseph
Chamberlain, suggest the possibility of carving out a Jewish
national homeland in East Africa. Herzl came to believe that
Africa might afford a temporary respite; referring to Palestine,
however, he declared, "If I forget thee, O Jerusalem, let my right

THEODORE HERZL

A Hungarian Jew born Into a prosperous family in 1860, Theodore Herzl
(1860–1904) was strongly influenced by the Germanic culture that dominated the Habsburg Empire. As a teenager, he wrote a series of plays about
the angst (anguish) suffered by young aristocrats, who were battling, as Herzl
had believed he was, against decadent bourgeois (middle-class) ways. The
emergence in Austria of anti-Semitism—which was adopted by his frater-
nity—troubled the young lawyer, who completed his formal education at the
University of Vienna in 1884. After working for the government for a short
spell, Herzl decided to become a full-time writer, ending up as a journalist in
Paris for the *Neue Freie Presse*, a leading Viennese newspaper.

Increasingly, Herzl began examining anti-Semitism more fully in his writing, including through his newspaper column. Mass conversion and socialism initially cropped up as two solutions for Herzl, but neither appeared
wholly satisfactory. In 1895, he published *Out of the Ghetto*, a play whose
Herzl-like protagonist was shot down in a duel with a Christian aristocrat.
The Dreyfus case in Paris, which resulted in the humiliation of a Jewish military officer wrongly accused of treason, heightened Herzl's desire to seek a
solution to the problem of anti-Semitism. Veiwing France, purportedly the
most enlightened European state, afflicted with the scourge, Herzl came to

hand wither." Other Zionists, however, demanded that a Jewish state be created in Palestine.[21]

Following Herzl's death in 1904, the Chovevei Zion, who remained committed to the idea of a Jewish Palestine, spearheaded the Zionist movement. From its inception, the Zionist movement viewed the *yishuv* (the Jewish community in Palestine) as "a territorial political entity, a united, autonomous, and democratic community,"[22] according to Eli Barnavi. A second aliyah migrated to Palestine from 1904 to 1914, with many newcomers, including the young David Ben-Gurion, desiring to create a socialist agricultural haven. Aided by the Jewish National Fund, the *Poale Zion* (Workers of Zion) and *Hapoel Hatzair* (The Young Worker) set up a series of communally run

believe that Jewish nationhood was necessary. Seeking to influence Baron Maurice de Hirsch, a wealthy Jewish philanthropist, among others, Herzl wrote a manifesto, *Der Judenstaat* (*The Jewish State*), which he hoped would be distributed around the world. Willpower alone, Herzl believed, had enabled Jews to survive for thousands of years, and that determination was rooted in core beliefs.

Herzl soon became a dominant figure in the Zionist movement, helping to convene the First Zionist Congress in Switzerland and to found the World Zionist Organization in 1897. Herzl contended that the establishment of a Jewish state would lead to the emergence of a new group of Jews who could be likened to the Maccabees. In public, Herzl argued that Jewish immigration to Palestine would not result in a displacement of Arab inhabitants, but behind the scenes, he admitted that expropriation and transference of the native population would occur. Relying on political or diplomatic Zionism, Herzl strove diligently to garner support from first the Turkish and then the British governments. Various English officials appeared increasingly receptive to the idea of a Jewish state featuring arbitrary borders of some sort; however, they talked about locating that state, at least temporarily, outside Palestine. His political maneuverings proved costly to his health, and Herzl died at the age of 44. In 1949, his remains were removed to Palestine for burial on Jerusalem's Mount Herzl.

agricultural settlements. The Russian Zionist Aaron David Gordon propounded the notion that physical labor was emancipatory. In 1910, Jewish settlers formed the first *kibbutz*, Degania, where the land, houses, and farming implements were owned in common. In the face of mounting Arab resentment, the Jewish population in Palestine reached 85,000 by 1914.

Throughout this period, the majority of the Arab population remained Sunni Muslims, with about one-sixth of Arabs being Christian, most of them Greek Orthodox. Establishing arbitrary borders, the Ottoman Turks had split Palestine into a northern sector, which was tied to Beirut, and a southern sector, centered on Jerusalem, but Palestine was generally viewed as being apart from Syria. After initially calling for Palestine's unification in 1872, the Ottomans changed their mind, fearing that such action would only enable Europeans to made deeper inroads. The Ottomans also viewed Zionists with concern, worrying that Jews would no longer accept dhimmi status within the empire. In fact, Muslims came to consider Zionism another Western imperialist movement that threatened Arab lands. At the same time, Jewish immigrants were still admitted as "scattered groups throughout the Ottoman Empire," but not to Palestine.[23] Increasingly, however, Jews purchased land in Palestine, despite prohibitions against foreigners doing so. In 1905, Naguib Azoury published *Le Reveil de la Nation Arabe* (*The Awakening of the Arab Nation*), which warned against "the hidden effort of the Jews to restore on a very large scale the ancient kingdom of Israel."[24]

World War I, which induced the Turkish government to expel 20,000 Jewish immigrants from Palestine, resulted in the British occupation of Ottoman territory, including Palestine, and further inspired the hope of Zionists for a Jewish national home there. This was hardly pleasing to the Arabs, who had been encouraged to battle against the Turks with at least the implicit promise of Arab independence tendered by British officials. According to the Sykes-Picot Agreement carved out with France, Palestine was to be placed under international control, with the

The Zionist movement, a campaign to acquire a separate Jewish homeland where the Hebrew language and Jewish culture could thrive, began in the late nineteenth century after repeated outbreaks of violent anti-Semitism. This photograph shows a group of Zionists delegates, including the founder of modern Zionism, Theodore Herzl (above, second row, center).

British taking over the ports of Haifa and Acre. Beginning in 1916, greater attention was paid to both Palestine and Zionism once David Lloyd George became prime minister. Strongly encouraged by Chaim Weizmann, a Russian-born Zionist who had immigrated to England—and hoping to engender support for the Allied war effort—the new government issued the Balfour Declaration on November 2, 1917. That document indicated, "His Majesty's Government view [sic] with favour the establishment in Palestine of a national home for the Jewish people," which would require the setting of arbitrary borders.[25] That proclamation also indicated, "Nothing shall be done which may prejudice the civil and religious rights of existing non-Jewish communities in Palestine, or the rights and political status enjoyed by Jews in any other country."[26]

During this same period, the British sought to placate Sheriff Hussein of Mecca, who opposed the establishment of a Jewish state in Palestine. After the end of World War I, however, the British appeared to back the idea of a Jewish homeland more strongly, with Lord Arthur Balfour acknowledging, "We conceive the Jews to have an historic claim to a home in their ancient land."[27] Although he was hoping that this could happen "without either dispossessing or oppressing the present inhabitants," Balfour insisted that Zionism's historic traditions were "of far profounder import than the desires and prejudices of the 700,000 Arabs who now inhabit that ancient land."[28] The failure to designate borders, however, demonstrated Balfour's recognition of the arbitrary nature of carving out a Jewish state, to which he had become increasingly sympathetic.

The League of Nations, founded in 1919, granted Great Britain mandatory rights in Palestine while reaffirming the Balfour Declaration and requiring its implementation in the Mandate Charter. Alarmed by the outbreak of armed resistance by Arabs, British colonial secretary Winston Churchill granted Abdullah ibn Husayn control over eastern Palestine, which became known as Trans-Jordan and had its own reshaped borders, notwithstanding objections by Zionists. It was anticipated that Jews would take control of western Palestine, but these possibilities failed to satisfy either Arabs or Jews.

From 1919 to 1923, a third aliyah unfolded, made up mostly of young socialist workers. More than 18,000 entered Palestine during the first three years; along with the previous aliyah, this one produced more kibbutzim and a series of *moshavim*. To defend the yishuv from attacks by Arabs, the *Haganah* was formed in 1920. Various clashes broke out in May 1921, resulting in scores of fatalities and the decision by Herbert Samuel, a Zionist who was acting as civilian governor of Palestine, to halt Jewish immigration. The British government offered a White Paper in mid-1922, indicating that Great Britain did "not contemplate that Palestine as a whole should be converted into a Jewish National Home, but that such a home should be founded in Palestine."[29] Thus, the very idea of a Jewish homeland, at least in the eyes of British officials, remained vague. Nevertheless, Jewish immigration continued, with some 65,000 Polish immigrants entering the territory known as Palestine between 1924 and 1927.

For his part, Weizmann helped establish a new Zionist group, the Jewish Agency, which he led. This group was headquartered in Jerusalem. Weizmann also took charge of the World Zionist Organization but increasingly battled with various groups in Palestine, including those guided by Ben-Gurion. The Palestinian Zionists were divided themselves, with Orthodox Jews opposing Zionism; Jewish entrepreneurs, who employed Arab workers, having no desire to be associated with the Zionists; and labor Zionists, fervently believing in socialism. The labor Zionists further splintered into Poale Zion, a group that Ben-Gurion championed and that sought to reach out to the majority of immigrants who dwelled in urban areas, and Hapoel Hatzair, a group influenced by David Gordon that envisioned collective settlements as the foundation for a new Jewish state. By 1920, *Histadrut*, a new labor confederation, appeared, which Ben-Gurion came to head; eventually, Histadrut became the leading organizational force in Jewish Palestine. A new party, the *Mapai*, appeared in late 1930, favoring a socialist perspective.

Opposing the labor Zionists were the supporters of Vladimir Jabotinsky, a charismatic Russian Jew and Zionist who, after World War I, helped defend Jews against Arab attacks in Jerusalem. Favoring private investment and immigration by middle-class Jews, Jabotinsky condemned labor Zionism "as a cancer on the national body politic."[30] Jabotinsky particularly appealed to young European Jews; they joined his youth groups or *Betar*, whose brown shirts and special salutes appeared to duplicate those of Hitler's Nazis or Mussolini's fascists. Rejecting any possibility of compromising with the Arabs, Jabotinsky and his Revisionists called for a united Jewish Palestine with expansive borders, which would include Trans-Jordan.

Throughout the 1920s, Jewish organizational efforts in

Palestine superseded those of the Arabs. Allowed to serve along-side British soldiers, Jews transferred weapons to the Haganah and acquired more through smuggling enterprises. Benefiting from access to outside funds, something Arabs lacked, Jews purchased more land in Palestine, first from absentee landlords but increasingly from financially strapped Arab peasants. All the while, the British spent a good amount of money on education, medical care, and the basic infrastructure, while the Zionist movement provided financial backing for technological developments, including electrification. Clearly then, hope existed that economic support could help reshape borders in the Middle East.

Conflicts mounted because of economic, religious, and territorial considerations. Jews considered the Western, or Wailing, Wall, where the first and second temples had resided in Old Jerusalem, to be their most sacred site; Arabs, on the other hand, revered the *Al-Haram Al-Sharif*, or Temple Mount, Islam's third holiest spot, and believed that the Wall was where Muhammad had ascended to heaven. Jews demanded control of the Wall, which was under the control of Muslims, something the British had supported. A clash ensued in August 1929, leading to Arab attacks on Jewish quarters in Jerusalem and elsewhere, with Zionist groups responding in kind. The killing of more than 200 people within a week resulted in the publication in early 1930 of the Shaw Report, which blamed Arabs for the violence but warned, "A landless and discontented class is being created," suggesting the need to restrict land sales.[31] The British government, led by Prime Minister Ramsey MacDonald, rejected the findings of a subsequent White Paper, which also called for curbing Jewish immigration.

Consequently, immigration to Palestine increased, with the Jewish population doubling between 1933 and 1935 alone, the period when Adolph Hitler and other virulent anti-Semites solidified their brutal hold on Germany. The Nazis, of course, sought to establish a caste system based on racial boundaries, with Jews and other denigrated groups placed at the bottom of the hierarchy. Responding to the mounting terror in Central

Following World War I and the issuance of the Balfour Declaration announcing Britain's support for a Jewish state within Palestine, tens of thousands of Jewish immigrants entered Palestine. In this 1930 photograph, Jewish immigrants walk to Palestine.

Europe, a good number of the new immigrants to Palestine were Germans; many were Poles; and a large percentage were members of the middle class, who brought needed capital with them. The mushrooming Jewish population, the continued transfer of Arab lands, and the emergence of a new generation of Arab leaders—many tied to the anti-Zionist Hajj Amin al-Husayni, the mufti of Jerusalem—provided the backdrop for the Arab Revolt of 1936. The recently formed *Istiqlal* party urged pan-Arab unity to resolve the dilemma of the Palestinian Arabs. Various underground organizations appeared, including Holy War, which was led by Abd al-Qadir al-Husayni, that called for armed resistance.

The revolt, which began in mid-April and ended in early November, involved attacks on Jewish and British forces but also a general strike by Arab employees and a refusal to engage in commercial transactions with Jews. The eventual arrival of 20,000 British troops helped quash the uprising, which had been led by the Arab Higher Committee, as did diplomatic dealings by Arab states. Responding to the strife, the British colonial office sharply reduced the number of entry permits granted to Jewish emigrants. In addition, the Peel Commission Report, issued on July 7, 1937, adjudged the conflict between Jews and Arabs in Palestine "irrepressible" and incapable of being resolved within a unitary state.[32] Attempting to shape Middle Eastern borders, the report recommended that Jews receive approximately one-fifth of the landscape of Palestine, including the northern portion of the Galilee, the Jezreel Valley, and the coastal plain from the Lebanese border down to just below Jaffa. Arabs would control the rest of Palestine, including the Negev, the Gaza Strip, and the West Bank. The British were to retain an enclave, which would contain Jerusalem, Bethlehem, and a passage to the sea at Jaffa. In addition, the Peel Commission called for an "exchange of population," involving 225,000 Arabs and 1,250 Jews, to ensure that the new Jewish state possessed far more Jews than Arabs.[33]

In July 1937, the Arab Higher Committee refused to accept the recommendations, dismissing the call to partition Palestine and the proposed artificial boundaries; the Committee remained determined to cede nothing of permanence to Jewish settlers. A second, far bloodier Arab Revolt erupted, with British officials now targeted. Attacks against Jews led to retaliations by the Haganah and the *Irgun*, a Jewish splinter group that employed terrorist tactics. As war approached in Europe, British officials were determined to end the revolt, which lasted until 1939. Hoping to garner support from Arab nations, particularly Syria, Iraq, and Egypt, the British government now rejected the partition plan. The Woodhead Commission delivered a White Paper on November 8, 1938, indicating that the Galilee, Jerusalem, Bethlehem, Jaffa, and the Negev would remain in British hands. Under this latest plan, a much reduced Jewish state, with constricted artificial borders, would run along the Mediterranean coast from Zikhron Ya'akov to Tel Aviv, whereas an Arab nation, approximately six times its counterpart, would include the rest of Samaria and Judea, in addition to the Gaza Strip.

Confronting continued Arab resistance, the British government delivered new proposals. One called for holding Jewish immigration at 80,000 to 100,000 for the next 10 years, and a subsequent plan would have limited immigration to 75,000 over 5 years, while allowing for an independent Palestinian nation. With Arab opposition unabated, the British decided that if they had to offend one party, they would avoid offending the Arabs, not the Jews. On May 17, 1939, a new White Paper appeared, capping Jewish immigration at 75,000 for the following 5 years, after which point Arabs would determine if additional immigration should be permitted. The White Paper also sharply restricted the ability of Jews to purchase land in Palestine and called for an independent Palestinian state to be established within 10 years, if relations between Arabs and Jews made that feasible.

Influenced by rebels who warned, "The English to the sea and the Jews to the graves," the Arab Higher Committee again declined the offer, demanding that Jewish immigration be terminated immediately.[34] The Jewish Agency pointed out that the need for a Jewish homeland had never been greater, and the Jewish community in Palestine—now almost 30 percent of the population there—insisted that it would refuse to adhere to British policy. Various British politicians were not much happier, including Winston Churchill, who likened the White Paper to the infamous Munich Agreement, which resulted in Germany's carving up of Czechoslovakia. Thus, British attempts to devise arbitrary borders for an independent Palestine appeared increasingly futile.

As the effort to establish a Jewish homeland in Palestine proceeded, Jews and the British sought to devise solutions that required the setting of arbitrary borders. Fearing that the infusion of Jewish immigrants would result in the loss of additional territory, Palestinian Arabs remained opposed to the idea of a Jewish state, no matter how narrowly its boundaries might be drawn. With the number of Jewish immigrants mounting, so too did opposition by Arab leaders, who clearly feared that Zionists would continually claim more land as the Jewish population increased. Jewish leaders, for their part, had to contend with the horrors afflicting their European brethren, which seemed to underscore the very need for a Jewish nation.

4

World War II
and
Partition

As historian Bennie Morris notes, although the Russian pogroms (massacres) of the 1880s sparked the advent of modern Zionism, the worst horrific pogrom of all, the Nazi-orchestrated Holocaust, helped bring about Jewish nationhood. The new surge of support for a Jewish state followed the United Nations' unsuccessful attempt to support a binational solution for Palestine, notwithstanding previous unsuccessful attempts to usher in a compromise that would satisfy both Arab and Jewish nationalists. Nevertheless, such a campaign resulted from the outbreak of World War II, which soon sparked Hitler's determination to carry out the final solution involving the eradication of European Jewry.

Shortly after the official declaration of war in early September 1939, Chaim Weizmann and the Jewish Agency promised to support the British military campaign against Nazi Germany. For his part, David Ben-Gurion declared that Jews should "help the British in their war against Hitler as if there were no White Paper; we must resist the White Paper as if there were no war."[35] Within a matter of days, Ben-Gurion told the leaders of the Haganah that Zionists had received the Balfour Declaration because of World War I, and now they needed to establish a Jewish homeland. A small band of Jewish fighters, who made up the Stern gang, continued to insist on a stridently anti-British policy. The emergence of the war proved more perplexing to Middle Eastern Arabs, including those in Palestine. Viewing the British as pro-Zionist, many Arab leaders bitterly recalled the brutal manner in which the Arab Revolt of 1936–1939 had been suppressed.

During the early stages of World War II, illegal Jewish immigration to Palestine continued, to the dismay of those same Arab figures. Although some 40,000 Jews had skirted past British immigration officials from 1934 to 1938, and another 9,000 managed to do so before the war began, less than 16,000 additional illegal immigrants were able to accomplish that feat through the end of the war. Great Britain adopted sometimes heavy-handed tactics to stem the flow of Jews to Palestine. Scores were returned to their countries of origin. British officials reduced the annual quotas for legal immigration—arbitrary borders of a demographic stripe—by the number of those found to be entering Palestine illegally. Eventually, the British government sent boatloads of illegal immigrants to camps in Mauritius and Cyprus, resulting in bombing operations by the Haganah and the Stern Gang.

Although determined to restrict Jewish immigration to Palestine, Great Britain hoped to avoid antagonizing American Jews or the U.S. government. Such concerns, coupled with anger resulting from the pro-Axis stance of many Arabs, led to the failure to implement the provision in the 1939 White Paper calling for Arab self-rule and preeminence in Palestine by means of carefully drawn, though transparently arbitrary, borders. At the same time, Allied setbacks early in the war cemented Great Britain's determination to placate the Arabs in order that the Middle East, including Palestine, would not erupt in violence.

Reneging on the promises implicit in the White Paper convinced many Arabs to back the Axis powers, which only heightened British hostility. Amin al-Husayni, who had been forced into exile, exhorted Muslims to participate in a *jihad* (holy war) against the British. By 1941, al-Husayni was residing in Berlin, where he delivered pro-Axis radio propaganda and promised to trigger another large Arab revolt. In return, Hitler agreed to grant the Arabs independent states and to destroy Jewish Palestine. Al-Husayni urged Eastern European governments to prevent Jews from immigrating to the Middle East.

The wartime antics of al-Husayni infuriated British officials, including Prime Minister Winston Churchill, who condemned the 1939 White Paper. The service of more than 25,000 Palestinian Jews in the British army, on the other hand, pleased the British government. Those soldiers helped terminate fascist control of Syria and Lebanon and conduct military operations in Iraq. In 1941, the Haganah set up a new elite fighting force, the *Palmah*. Only late in the war did Churchill agree to the establishment of a Jewish brigade, something Zionists had desired.

Like the Zionists, Churchill recognized that the presence of veteran soldiers after the war might help safeguard the Jewish Palestinian community. Fearing that such forces could help the drive for a Jewish state, Arabs opposed establishment of the brigade. By late 1941, Churchill recognized how dramatically the war could affect Palestine and its artificial borders. Writing about the possibility of a victory by British and American forces, he suggested, "The creation of a great Jewish state in Palestine inhabitated [sic] by millions of Jews will be one of the leading features of the Peace Conference discussions."[36] As word of the full extent of the Holocaust mounted, Churchill appeared increasingly receptive to the idea of a Jewish nation.

Writing in *Foreign Affairs* magazine in January 1942, Chaim Weizmann insisted on the need for a Jewish state situated west of the Jordan River. That May, the Extraordinary Zionist Conference convening in New York supported the Biltmore program, which insisted that Palestine "be established as a Jewish Commonwealth integrated in the structure of the new democratic world ..."; still, the Jewish leaders who agreed to the program recognized that such a state would control only part of Palestine.[37] By August 1942, the Inner Zionist Greater Council in Jerusalem accepted the Biltmore program, although some were displeased with the notion that Palestine would not be fully Jewish.

With the encouragement of Churchill and Zionists, the British government, by mid-1943, began to reexamine its policy regarding the Middle East. That December, a cabinet committee reaffirmed the Peel Committee's call for partition, but the full cabinet failed to make a definitive decision. Then, members of *Lehi* (Fighters for the Freedom of Israel), derived from the Stern gang, murdered Lord Moyne, a good friend of the prime minister's, in Cairo. Speaking to the House of Commons, Churchill warned, "If our dreams for Zionism are to end in the smoke of assassins' pistols and our labours for its future to produce only a new set of gangsters worthy of Nazi Germany, many like myself will have to reconsider the position we have maintained so consistently in the past."[38] An angered Churchill now refused to champion the division of Palestine and the creation of new borders that would benefit the Zionists.

Although Weitzmann continued to support negotiations with the British regarding partition, both the Jewish Agency and the Yishuv's National Assembly demanded nationhood in all of Palestine. In fact, both Irgun, led by Menahem Begin—who headed Betar in Poland—and Lehi insisted on the creation of a Jewish state with expanded borders that arbitrarily contained Palestine, Trans-Jordan, and sections of Lebanon and Syria. Responding to British demands, the Haganah moved to reign in both Lehi and the Irgun, even delivering certain Irgun operatives to British policemen. This period consequently was known as the "hunting season."[39]

In the meantime, the Palestinian Arab leadership had experienced changes of its own. The termination of the Arab Revolt of 1936–1939 led to the disappearance of the Arab Higher Committee. The mufti (the Muslim cleric authorized to deliver rulings on religious issues) was officially banned from Palestine, and many Arab leaders also went into exile. At the beginning of the war, the British government sought the mufti's support for the White Paper and the restriction of Jewish immigration; the mufti, of course, had rejected such an overture, instead backing the Italian and German war campaigns. Other Arab figures did return to Palestine, having promised to avoid direct political involvement; they generally accepted the 1939 White Paper and helped prevent unrest from breaking out in Arab communities. Wartime prosperity, ironically resulting from British military occupation, served to placate many Arabs, if only temporarily. Nevertheless, Istiqlal members attempted to parlay the improved economic circumstances into intensified resistance to Zionism. The strengthened position of the Istiqlal displeased powerful clans, including the al-Husayni, who moved to reestablish the Palestine Arab party; in contrast to the Istiqlal, the Palestine Arab party rejected the presence of any Jews in Palestine, other than those whose families had resided there before 1917. A few thousand Arabs acquired military experience during the war, but little organizational improvement occurred.

A group of Arabian government leaders, gathered in Alexandria, Egypt, in October 1944, insisted, "It is second to none in regretting the woes that have been inflicted upon the Jews of Europe...." The resolution declared, "The question of these Jews should not be confused with Zionism, for there can be no greater injustice and aggression than solving the problem of the Jews of Europe by another injustice, that is, by inflicting injustice on the Palestine Arabs of various religions and denominations."[40] Emerging from the Alexandria conference, a League of Arab States encouraged President Franklin D. Roosevelt of the United States to agree that consultation with Arab leaders would predate any resolution of the Palestinian quandary. In November 1945, the Arab League reinstated the Arab Higher Committee, intending that it serve as the dominant political organization in Arab Palestine. Once again, the Husaynis took control of the Arab Higher Committee.

Significant changes of power had also occurred in both the United States and England. President Roosevelt died in April 1945, replaced by Harry S Truman, who appeared to support the Zionist position somewhat more than did his predecessor, although Roosevelt had earlier insisted that complete justice would be afforded to those who desired a Jewish homeland. In June, the British populace rejected Churchill's bid for another term as prime minister, replacing him with Clement Attlee of the Labor party. Foreign Secretary Ernest Bevin recognized that Great Britain was virtually bankrupted from the two world wars and was unable to maintain a major military presence in the Middle East. This suggested how difficult and expensive a proposition it was for outsiders like the British to attempt to draw artificial boundaries in the Middle East. Nevertheless, the British hoped to protect valuable oil interests in the region, along with control over the Suez Canal. That required, or so Bevin believed, the presence of British troops in Palestine.

The thought of British troops in Palestine displeased Zionists,

From the beginning, the establishment of a Jewish state in Palestine prompted constant, and often violent, controversy. Here, civilians walk through Jerusalem's business district after an explosion that was part of the warfare between Jews and Palestinians following the decision to partition Palestine.

who were also angered by Bevin's call for a return to the provisions established in the 1939 White Paper, which allowed for a monthly quota of 1,500 Jews to immigrate to Palestine. Weizmann refused to accept this figure, and President Truman also seemed desirous of a more generous policy. Earl G. Harrison, who headed Truman's Intergovernmental Committee on Refugees, pointed to Palestine as the ideal spot for the remnants of European Jewry, in the wake of the Holocaust. Thus, Truman requested that 100,000 Jews be admitted into Palestine, something the British government refused to consider.

Zionists were also upset that Bevin spoke of a future Palestinian state but not a Jewish one, to be established under a British-run trusteeship sanctioned by the United Nations.

Following the end of the war, the Haganah linked with the Irgun and Lehi to conduct a battle against the British position in Palestine. Responding quickly, Whitehall sent 80,000 troops to stifle the rebellion, which had resulted in the killing of several soldiers and policemen. In addition, Palmah sappers (demolition

THE JEWISH AGENCY

On August 11, 1929, the World Zionist Organization, holding the sixteenth Zionist congress, established the Jewish Agency to garner support from non-Zionist figures such as French socialist leader Leon Blum and the famed Jewish-American lawyer Louis Marshall. The Jewish Agency also intended to further the UN mandate for Palestine articulated seven years earlier, which called for the eventual transference to local populations of territories taken from defeated parties at the close of World War I. The Jewish Agency, which sought to bring about a Jewish national home in Palestine, came to be viewed as a de facto government representing Jews worldwide in their dealings with the League of Nations and the British mandate.

The Jewish Agency, led by David Ben-Gurion, attempted to persuade the British government, despite mounting Arab opposition, to allow a liberal policy pertaining to Jewish immigrants seeking entry into Palestine. At the same time, the organization controlled the Palestinian Jewish community's internal operations, ranging from the placement of immigrants to the construction of new settlements that would result in artificial boundaries pitting Jews against Arabs; by 1931, the Jewish Agency even directed the Haganah. As repression intensified in Hitler's Germany, the Jewish Agency worked to increase the outflow of immigrants to Palestine, spearheading a youth aliyah in 1934, which helped bring 5,000 young people to the Middle East. Beginning in the last half of the 1930s, with the Arab Revolt unfolding and the condition of European Jews plummeting, the Jewish Agency became involved in campaigns to foster illegal immigration to Palestine. After World War II, the Jewish Agency sent representatives to displaced persons camps in Europe while continuing to funnel illegal immigrants to Palestinian ports. In addition, the Jewish Agency helped build momentum for Jewish statehood, establishing a national council and a national administration after passage of a UN resolution that supported partition and the setting of arbitrary borders for Palestine.

specialists) blew up railway tracks, a British patrol vessel, and two British coast guard posts. On the evening of June 17, 1946, the "Night of the Bridges," Palmah operatives targeted 11 bridges that linked Palestine to its neighbors.[41] At the same time, the *Mossad le'Aliyah Bet* led an illegal immigration campaign, helping steer 65 vessels transporting 70,000 Jews to Palestine. International opposition to British policy mounted, thanks to reports of Jews—including many displaced persons who had endured the horrors of Nazi persecution—being forcibly interned in a detention camp on Cyprus.

A war of nerves continued between Zionists and the British, with the American government becoming increasingly concerned about developments in the Middle East and possible alterations of artificial boundaries in Palestine. Following World War II, when oil had proven to be such an invaluable asset for the Allies, British and U.S. government and corporate officials worried how regional tensions might affect oil reserves. In late June 1946, the British arrested members of the Jewish Executive Agency in Palestine. On July 22, in the midst of a cease-fire of sabotage operations, individuals affiliated with the Irgun and Lehi blew up Jerusalem's King David Hotel, which housed British military headquarters, killing 90, including both Jews and Arabs. The so-called Hebrew Resistance Movement splintered once again, with the Haganah denouncing terrorism. That October, new Jewish settlements were established in the Negev, and President Truman declared his support for partition and the establishment of a Jewish state.

Great Britain continued to confront pressure from both sides, which had contrasting visions of artificial boundaries: The Zionists insisted on partition, and the Arabs demanded all of Palestine and an immediate end to Jewish immigration. In February 1947, Bevin informed the House of Commons that Great Britain remained unable to resolve the dilemma on its own; he soon indicated that the United Nations would have to do so. All the while, the Irgun and Lehi increased the number of terrorist strikes waged against British forces. In late July, British

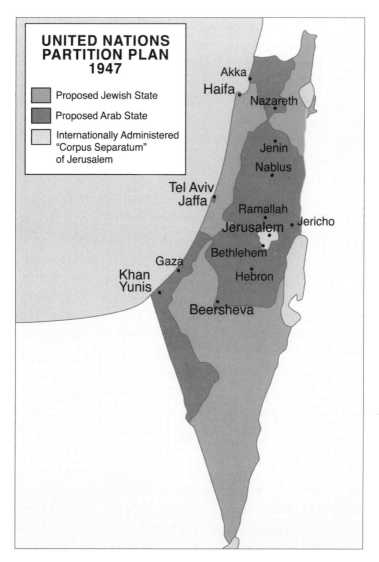

**UNITED NATIONS
PARTITION PLAN
1947**

Proposed Jewish State

Proposed Arab State

Internationally Administered
"Corpus Separatum"
of Jerusalem

Akka

Haifa

Nazareth

Jenin

Nablus

Tel Aviv
Jaffa

Ramallah

Jerusalem • Jericho

Bethlehem

Gaza

Khan
Yunis

Hebron

Beersheva

In 1947, the United Nations passed a resolution allowing Jews to construct an independent state in Palestine alongside an Arab state. This map shows the UN plan and the lands allotted to each group.

soldiers and policemen responded with a rampage through Tel Aviv that resulted in several deaths.

That same month witnessed the sailing of the *Exodus*, packed with 4,500 displaced persons, from southern France. British marines grabbed the boat and eventually towed it into Haifa, where most of the passengers were sent back to France on three ships. When the French refused to allow the boats to land, they went on to Hamburg, where British soldiers compelled them to disembark. The incidents surrounding the *Exodus* once again cost the British considerable goodwill within the international community.

During this same period, members of a special UN committee, instructed to explore conditions, spent time in Palestine, being well received by the Haganah but boycotted by Arab leaders. Committee members were present as Jews and the British conducted violent acts against one another, and they also spent time back in Europe, where they interviewed displaced persons. It was hardly surprising that the committee's report, released on September 1, urged that the British mandate cease. The majority recommendations also called for establishment of both a Jewish state and an Arab state in Palestine, which would require the determination of corresponding artificial frontiers, and the internationalization of Jerusalem and Bethlehem. The minority report urged that a larger Palestine become an independent, federal state, dominated by Arabs.

Prior to a vote in the UN's General Assembly, the British cabinet voted in September to terminate the mandate and withdraw from Palestine. There was extensive lobbying by Zionists in the United States to convince President Truman to support the partition plan, as the Soviets had recently done. In early October, both the United States and the Soviet Union publicly declared support for a two-state plan. Weizmann convinced Truman to oppose the granting of the Negev to the Arabs, an action the State Department favored. For its part, the Jewish Agency allowed Beersheba and land alongside the border between the Sinai and the Negev to be included in the proposed Arab state. Under the plan, which the United Nations considered on November 29, the Jewish nation was to hold a slight majority of the Palestinian landscape, along with a population of 900,000, a half-million of whom were Jews.

With considerable pressure by the United States and support by the Soviet bloc, UN Resolution 181 passed; the international body thereby acknowledged the right of Jews to establish an independent state in Palestine with its own boundary lines, side-by-side with an Arab state. Announcement of the decision elated Zionists but infuriated Arabs, whose leaders denounced the UN provision as illegitimate. Ben-Gurion happily responded, "I know of no greater achievement by the Jewish people ... in its long history since it became a people." Arab representatives reacted differently, failing to comprehend "why it was *not* fair for the Jews to be a minority in a unitary Palestinian state, while it *was* fair for almost half of the Palestinian population—the indigenous majority on its own ancestral soil—to be converted overnight into a minority under alien rule."[42]

Once again, stark differences separated Jews and Arabs, in spite of elaborately constructed efforts to establish a workable compromise regarding Palestine. UN Resolution 181 involved such an effort and sought to create separate Jewish and Arab states on Palestinian soil. UN representatives diligently strove to shape those states by establishing arbitrary borders, but to little avail. Although Zionist leaders appeared willing to accept the Jewish state as created, no matter how narrow its boundaries, their Arab counterparts viewed that development with fear and dismay.

5

The 1948–1949
Arab-Israeli War

During the summer of 1947, leaders of the Arab nations surrounding Palestine privately acknowledged their inability to stave off the construction of a Jewish nation, if the UN supported the partition plan. By contrast, the Palestinian Arab Higher Committee decided to resort to military action, beginning on November 30, one day following the UN's passage of Resolution 181, which championed the partitioning of Palestine. Like the Palestinian Arabs, Zionists recognized that resorting to arms was inevitable and moved to grab territory in the Galilee, along the coast, and in the hills of Judea. As Derek J. Penslar suggests, "The partition borders," which established arbitrary boundaries for Palestine, "were a strategic nightmare."[43] To the Haganah, this required immediate expansion into territories throughout Palestine, including Galilee, the coastal area, and the hills of Judea.

In accepting Resolution 181, the Zionists seemingly acquiesced to the creation of an Arab Palestinian state with its own artificial borders that would incorporate all the territory not set aside for the Jewish nation. They, like British officials and Jordan's King Abdullah, however, hardly viewed such a development with favor. Abdullah sought control of the territory that was to make up a Palestinian state; both the Zionists, who had been engaged in negotiations with Abdullah since the end of the war, and the British considered such a possibility preferable to the likelihood of more militant Palestinians governing that land.

In early December 1947, the Arab Higher Committee supported a general strike, which soon resulted in violent outbreaks in Jerusalem, near Tel Aviv, and in a series of towns across Palestine. The Irgun and Lehi employed terrorist actions, including the tossing of bombs at Arabs working near an oil refinery in Haifa. After six Arabs died, Arab laborers inside the gates of the plant murdered 41 Jews before British soldiers responded. A short while afterward, Haganah agents moved into a village close to Haifa and killed about 60 people, including a large number of women and children. Bombings in urban areas drove out some 15,000 Arabs. By January, Syrian and Egyptian members of the

Arab Liberation Army (ALA) entered Palestine, helping to isolate Jerusalem and a series of Jewish settlements. The Palmah experienced several casualties while attempting to protect those Jewish pockets. Nevertheless, the Irgun carried out operations in Palestine's largest cities, which resulted in hundred of Arab fatalities and injuries. Both sides conducted raids against convoys.

Although the Palestinian Arab population was double that of the Jews, the Palestinians lacked the level of organization and even the tradition of public service that their foes boasted. The Arab Higher Committee remained unrepresentative of the Palestinian Arabs, suffered from corruption, and sought to guide a people lacking much in the way of government or military experience. The Yishuv was very politically conscious and benefited from the existence of a quasi-state infrastructure, which included the Haganah, the Jewish Agency, settlement agencies, and Histadrut, the potent labor confederation. Additionally, the Palestinian Jews received support from the World Zionist Organization, which helped provide necessary financial resources for the Yishuv. In early 1948, supporters promised Golda Meir $50 million for the Haganah. Significantly, many Jewish settlements were, in effect, military fortresses, but the Haganah possessed no artillery, tanks, or combat planes and very little ammunition.

Lacking any national military apparatus, the Palestinian Arabs relied on a series of military bands that cropped up early in the war. The most noteworthy Arab military unit was Fawzi al Qawuqji's ALA, which drew heavily from Syrian volunteers, but the Palestinians usually relied on small militia units. During the first few months of fighting, the Arabs appeared to be on the offensive, whereas the Haganah adopted a largely defensive posture. Militia forces, conducting commando strikes, serving as snipers, and employing bombs, produced hundreds of Jewish casualties while attacking isolated rural settlements and Jerusalem, where the food supply was becoming critical and riots appeared imminent.

These developments, coupled with concerns about when UN

peacekeepers might replace British forces, led the Haganah—which suffered a series of devastating setbacks in late March—to change its strategy. The Haganah, which began to operate more like a regular army, received desperately needed arms from Czechoslovakia in early April. With British troops departing, the Haganah began to take control of wider swaths of territory, thus altering boundary lines, as Ben-Gurion insisted that the Jewish sectors of Jerusalem be held through Operation *Nahshon*. On April 8, a Jewish sentry shot Abd al-Quadir al-Husayni, who was commanding Palestinian militias around Jerusalem. The next morning, an Irgun and Lehi cadre, with backing by the Haganah, attacked the village of Dayr Yasin. Although the Jewish forces suffered a handful of fatalities, they carried out a wholesale massacre, killing some 100 to 110 Arabs, many of whom had been robbed and were eventually mutilated.

The Jewish Agency condemned the operation, which was publicized by the Irgun and Lehi to terrorize Arabs; by the Haganah to castigate its rivals; and by Arabs and the British to despoil the image of Jewish fighters. In an act of retaliation, Arabs murdered 70 doctors and nurses from a convoy that was heading to Hadassah Hospital and Hebrew University on Mount Scopus. Nevertheless, fears of additional attacks by the Irgun and Lehi resulted in mass departures of Arabs from various villages and from Haifa. In the north, attacks by the Haganah led *Druze* (an offshoot of *Ismaili Shi'i* Muslims) units to withdraw from the ALA and establish more conciliatory relations with Jewish forces, which had a lasting impact. Jewish fighters took control of Tiberias, Haifa, the Manshiya district in Jaffa, and the Katamon district in Jerusalem, within a two-week span. Safad fell by May 12, with an Arab exodus spurred by psychological warfare, while Jews grabbed hold of all eastern Galilee. Altogether, some 300,000 Arabs fled their homes by mid-May. Arab propaganda suggested that a quick return to departed villages and cities would follow a military victory over the Jews, whereas Zionists welcomed the departure of large numbers of Arabs. When some Arabs sought to return to Haifa, which the Jewish mayor had encouraged, the Haganah turned down their requests. Jews suffered setbacks of their own, with four settlements near Hebron taken over by Arab militiamen and Arab legionnaires, who killed more than 100 residents and took about 350 prisoners.

Nevertheless, the Zionists clearly possessed the upper hand after nearly half a year of fighting. They now controlled significant parcels of territory previously assigned to the Palestinians or placed under international auspices through the creation of earlier artificial boundaries, and they held the coastal strip, the Jezreel Valley, and the Jordan Valley; the Arabs controlled Galilee, Samaria, and Judea. The Haganah had acquired invaluable military experience, which served it well once a new stage of warfare began. After the British pulled out the last of their troops, Ben-Gurion, in the late afternoon of May 14, spoke at the Tel Aviv Museum:

> The Land of Israel was the birthplace of the Jewish people. Here their spiritual, religious and national identity was formed. Here they achieved independence and created a culture of national and universal significance. Here they wrote and gave the Bible to the world.
>
> Exiled from Palestine, the Jewish people remained faithful to it in all the countries of their dispersion, never ceasing to pray and hope for their return and the restoration of their national freedom....
>
> We, the members of the National Council, representing the Jewish people in Palestine and the Zionist movement of the world ... by virtue of the natural and historic right of the Jewish people and of the resolution of the General Assembly of the United Nations, hereby proclaim the establishment of the Jewish state in Palestine, to be called Israel.[44]

Both the United States and the Soviet Union quickly recognized the new nation with its seemingly ever-shifting borders, whose first prime minister was Ben-Gurion; the ceremonial position of president was held by Chaim Weitzmann. In the midst of such diplomatic successes and general jubilation expe-

Despite protests from Arab Palestinians, the Jewish state of Israel became a nation in 1948. Here, Israeli Prime Minister David Ben-Gurion and Israeli Foreign Minister Moshe Sharett sign a document declaring Jewish independence.

rienced by many Jews worldwide, Haganah leaders warned President Ben-Gurion that Israel had only a 50-50 chance of warding off invading Arab armies. On May 15, the very day word was received that the Americans and Soviets would recognize the Jewish state, Israel came under attack from Arab nations. Iraq, Syria, Lebanon, Egypt, Jordan, and Saudi Arabia sent forces into the territory that had made up prewar Palestine.

The IDF could call on 42,000 armed men and women and had a bounty of small arms, and it soon produced sufficient submachine guns, mortars, antitank rockets, and explosive devices. Initially lacking heavy weapons, the Haganah stole or purchased a number of tanks, armored vehicles, and patrol vessels from the British. Possessing fewer than 30 light airplanes and lacking combat aircraft altogether, the Haganah soon purchased four Czech fighter planes and attempted to outfit some of its own aircraft. The Arab contingents included 28,000 troops but seemingly had at their disposal far more combat aircraft, tanks, armored vehicles, and antiaircraft weaponry than the Israelis. Much of that war material, however, never became available during the second stage of the Arab-Israeli War.

Once this phase of the fighting began, both sides markedly augmented their forces; the IDF had 65,000 soldiers by mid-July and 115,000 by the following spring. Their Arab opponents in Palestine and Sinai numbered 40,000 by mid-July and 55,000 by October. Also key to the Israeli victory was the ability to overcome a UN-sponsored arms embargo that lasted from late May 1948 through August 1949; the United States had established its own embargo in December 1947, and the British did so in February 1948. Unlike the Arab states, the Israelis devised a large-scale arms network in both Europe and the Western Hemisphere; of $129 million obtained from Jews residing overseas, more than 60 percent was spent to purchase arms. The Israelis were also aided by thousands of volunteers, both Jews and Gentiles alike, who assisted the IDF, particularly helping to provide invaluable air supremacy.

The lack of coordination among the Arab states also helped determine the war's outcome. So too did overconfidence that the Jews would be driven into the sea. Hardly helping matters was the fact that Jordan's King Abdullah was most interested in taking control of the West Bank, had little interest in Palestine's northern sector, and largely deployed his Arab legion forces, the toughest competitors for the Israelis, in a defensive mode. Moreover, Abdullah, who had secretly been negotiating with the Jewish Agency for two years, had appeared to suggest before the war's outbreak that Jordan would accept the existence of a Jewish state with even broader boundaries than existed when the war began.

Intense fighting occurred during the first two weeks of the war, with the Haganah enduring large casualties; the kibbutzim Sha'ar Ha'Golan, Massadah, and Mishmar Hayarden fell to the Syrians; the Arab legion conquered the Jewish Quarter in Old

Jerusalem; and the Egyptians took Yad Mordechai. At the same time, the Israelis saddled the Arab legion with heavy losses, leading Abdullah to worry that his army might disintegrate and the West Bank fall. The Israelis also conducted aerial strikes against both Amman and Damascus before a four-week long truce, orchestrated by Swedish Count Folke Bernadotte of the United Nations. In an effort to reign in militias outside the Haganah, Ben-Gurion demanded that the Irgun and Lehi disband. In one incident, the Haganah fired on a ship, the *Altalena*, which carried weapons and Irgun volunteers, resulting in the sinking of the boat and the death of 18 men.

In late June, UN mediator Bernadotte called for the division of Palestine into two states with arbitrary borders, similar to those proposed by Resolution 181, fitted within a federal confederation. Under Bernadotte's plan, a Jewish state would contain western Galilee but not the Negev; an Arab state would include the West Bank. After two years, the United Nations would determine what to do about Jewish immigration, and Arabs would be permitted to return to the domiciles they had fled. Haifa, like Lydda Airport, was to be internationalized, and Jews in Jerusalem were to possess municipal autonomy inside an Arab-dominated region. The Arabs dismissed Bernadotte's plan as amounting to the partition plan they had previously rejected; Israelis believed that the events of the war would enable them to garner more generous terms. This graphically demonstrated once more how even well-intentioned attempts by outsiders to establish arbitrary boundaries in the Middle East invariably failed.

The war began again on July 8, resulting in an Egyptian offensive and a counterstrike by the IDF. During the 10 days of this new phase of the conflict, the Israeli forces generally held the initiative, particularly in the northern and central sectors. Israeli planes also bombed Cairo and Damascus before a second truce was called, which lasted through mid-October. The Syrian, Jordanian, and Iraqi forces remained on the sidelines after July 18. On September 18, members of Lehi assassinated

UN mediator Bernadotte in Jerusalem, which he had sought to internationalize; the American Ralph Bunche replaced him. The Israelis took advantage of the cease-fire to build up their forces, acquiring a greater numerical superiority over their foes. They also now possessed much more impressive military hardware than before, including a large number of armored vehicles, artillery pieces, heavy mortars, antiaircraft and antitank weapons, fighter planes, and bombers.

When the war resumed, the Israelis concentrated their firepower against Egypt, which most imperiled Tel Aviv and Jewish settlements in the Negev. Ben-Gurion had urged his fellow cabinet members to support a move to take the entire Judea-Hebron area, which included East Jerusalem and Bethlehem. The majority of the cabinet, however, feared the possibility of involving Israeli soldiers in a battle against their British counterparts because Great Britain had carved out a defense treaty with Jordan; those cabinet members also worried that Israel, should it control the West Bank and its geographic boundaries, would thereby take on more than 500,000 more Arabs. The Israelis worried that such expanded borders would compel the Jewish state to take responsibility for a potentially volatile, mixed population.

Israeli units attacked the Egyptians on October 15; Beersheba was taken within 5 days, and a series of kibbutzim were recaptured. As the Egyptians suffered a rout, the IDF also prevailed in the central and northern sections of the Galilee, pummeling ALA forces, which never rebounded from their latest setbacks. Near the end of the month, the IDF retook al-Malikiya, which had fallen to ALA and Lebanese forces. On October 31, Israeli soldiers swept through 15 villages north of the Lebanese border, advancing to the Litani River. Benny Morris suggests that the IDF conducted a series of massacres involving both Palestinian noncombatants and prisoners of war.

After another lull in the fighting, the Israelis decided to take hold of large expanses of territory then remaining in Egyptian hands but which UN Resolution 181 had earmarked for a Jewish state and its boundary lines. Beginning on December 19, the IDF conducted a major offensive to push the Egyptians out of Palestine. On December 28, the Israelis crossed the international border—itself artificial—to head into Sinai, to the chagrin of the British, who had a defense treaty with Egypt. At year's end, a U.S. special representative delivered an admonition from President Truman to Israeli Foreign Minister Moshe Sharett. The British, for their part, spoke of ending their arms embargo to the Arab states. Although the IDF pulled back from the Sinai, Egypt soon faced another offensive in the north, beginning on January 3, 1949. As the Egyptian expeditionary force faced encirclement, Western nations again protested that Israel had violated international boundaries.

On January 5, Egypt, fearing that its army could be crushed altogether, declared its readiness to engage in armistice talks should the Israeli offensive end. Worried about international pressure and the possible loss of additional U.S. financial backing, the Israeli government supported an immediate cessation of hostilities and the initiation of armistice talks regarding peace and the establishment of new borders. Just prior to the start of discussions in Rhodes on January 12, Israeli planes blasted five British warplanes.

Although various Israeli troop movements would continue over the next two months, the 1948–1949 Arab-Israeli War had largely come to an end. By early March, the new Jewish state occupied the central and southern Negev, reaching to Aqaba, as well as a good portion of the western side of the Dead Sea, as had been promised under UN Resolution 181. The Jewish community in Israel had paid a heavy price, suffering 6,000 fatalities. The Arab loss of life proved difficult to determine but undoubtedly also numbered in the thousands. Jordan acquired control over the West Bank, with its restive Palestinian population; Egypt held the Gaza Strip, which also contained a large pool of unhappy Palestinians. Altogether, at least 600,000 Palestinians became refugees, creating a social and political problem that immediately festered. Equally striking, Palestine's arbitrary borders had shifted dramatically.

In the process, the Green Line, which encircled Israel after the close of the war, had come into existence. Israel had greatly increased its territorial holdings but had also acquired hostile neighbors, particularly Egypt to the south, Syria to the north, and Jordan to the east. The Green Line demonstrated all too dramatically how the drawing of arbitrary borders in the area long known as Palestine remained in flux. Even the establishment of the Jewish state failed to create stable, permanent borders, particularly because both Arabs and Jews considered the Green Line to be temporary. Many Arabs refused to recognize Israel's existence, whereas a number of Jews desired control of even larger swaths of territory, with some hearkening back to biblical injunctions that purportedly established boundaries for a Jewish nation.

6

War Between
the Wars

The armistice agreements officially terminated the 1948–1949 Arab-Israeli War and created the Green Line surrounding Israel but produced mixed results. Israel now held a much larger amount of territory than had been proposed under UN Resolution 181, which had attempted to establish new artificial boundaries for Palestine by creating both an Arab nation and a Jewish nation. The United Nations sought to do so through diplomatic persuasion, but the refusal of Arab nations to accept the resolution led to military conflict, which eventually culminated in the creation of the state of Israel, with expanded borders. Significantly, Jerusalem stood as a divided city, with Israel and Jordan controlling different sectors. No Palestinian nation emerged from the war, with both Egypt and Jordan holding land that was supposed to have been part of that state. Hundreds of thousands of Palestinian refugees now existed, creating a social, political, and economic dilemma of considerable proportions. Moreover, the armistice pacts did not result in peace treaties, and thus a state of perpetual hostility existed. So too did concerns about the Green Line, whose very existence enraged Palestinian Arabs and Arab countries.

Located within the Green Line, the new state of Israel stood as a parliamentary democracy rooted in western ideals, whose Declaration of Independence promised to "guarantee freedom of religion, conscience, language, education and culture."[45] Although many of its socialist founders, including David Ben-Gurion, had envisioned a secular state, the prime minister felt compelled to carve out an alliance between his own organization, the Mapai, and the religious bloc that could wield the balance of power in Israel's multiparty government. In return for secular control of political and diplomatic affairs, Ben-Gurion agreed to allow orthodox rabbis to preside over marriages and divorces, to have public transportation restricted on the Sabbath, and to have the Israeli army adhere to kosher dietary laws. Not everyone was pleased with this compromise, and other controversies developed concerning the question of "Who is a Jew?" within the borders of the Jewish state.

Thus, the Israelis wrestled with another kind of artificial boundary—that involving religion, ethnicity, nationality, and culture—the very kind of boundary Jews had long been forced to contend with. In the previous century, for a time, it had appeared that the Jewish enlightenment and a new, more liberal age might break down such artificial barriers, but other, far more dangerous ones had been enacted, leading to the terror of the Holocaust. Now, Jews again wrestled with the question of identity, in sometimes ironic fashion, given what so many associated with the faith had recently endured.

Meanwhile, Israel's Jewish population continued to grow, encouraged by the Law of Return, announced in 1950, which declared, "Every Jew had the right to immigrate to the country." Within four years of the beginning of statehood, the number of Jews inside Israel and the Green Line more than doubled, as almost 700,000 immigrants arrived, mostly from Europe or other Middle Eastern countries. A large number of the new European refugees were destitute, lacking skills and financial resources. The growing hostility encountered by Jews in Arab states, exemplified by anti-Jewish riots, induced many to immigrate to Israel. Some 45,000 came from Yemen alone over a 14-month time span, beginning in June 1949. By 1952, almost 125,000 Iraqi Jews arrived, and many also came from Iran, Algeria, Tunisia, Morocco, and Libya. They, too, tended to be poor, requiring public assistance. That in turn resulted in tremendous pressures falling on Zionist organizations to garner financial support, particularly from the United States. By 1953, a decision was made to amend the Law of Return to allow Israel to deny admission to the aged, the infirm, or the indigent.

Tensions arose as the demographic composition of Israel changed, seemingly pitting Ashkenazic Jews against Sephardic newcomers. The Ashkenazim, with their European origins, had long dominated the Zionist movement and included most of Israel's founders and the majority of its Jewish population when the state was created. The 300,000 Sephardim from Middle Eastern states, who came to Israel during its early years, were often shuffled off to transit camps and saw their traditions viewed as "primitive" by the Ashkenazim.[46] Eventually, many Sephardim settled in new communities in far-flung areas or in dilapidated urban neighborhoods.

By 1950, inside Israel, within the Green Line and its extended arbitrary borders, there also dwelled approximately 170,000 Arabs, who were frequently viewed with suspicion although they were accorded Israeli citizenship under the Law of Nationality. Many resided on lands close to the Green Line established through the 1949 armistice agreements; those areas were labeled military zones, where mandates enforced by the IDF prevailed. Thus, residents could be removed from various areas and their property confiscated. Military edicts could result in the relocation of entire villages and their replacement by Jewish ones. More than a half-million Palestinians dwelled in Jordan, which was the lone Arab nation to grant them citizenship. Many Palestinians still could be found in refugee camps that the United Nations Relief and Works Agency (UNRWA) funded. About 200,000 Palestinians lived in the Gaza Strip; almost 100,000 were in Lebanon, and another 60,000 went to Syria. The bulk of Palestinians resided in refugee camps, with many refusing to be resettled. Arab heads of state insisted on the right of Palestinian refugees to return to the homes and land they had left. Israel countered that Arab nations, with their own borders so arbitrarily drawn, should incorporate the Palestinians just as it was accepting Jews from throughout the Middle East.

Hostilities continued between Israel and her Arab neighbors, with the Arab League establishing an economic boycott in January 1950. That same month witnessed the proclamation by the Israeli government that Jerusalem was the capital of the Jewish state. From 1951 to 1956, approximately 3,000 armed confrontations and 6,000 acts of sabotage occurred within Israel's boundaries inside the Green Line, leading to the deaths of more than 400 Israelis. Most of the clashes occurred in the demilitarized zones (DMZs) along the borders, where Israeli territory

Hostility and violence between Israel and the Arab nations intensified, despite peacemaking efforts by leading Western powers. Thousands of armed confrontations and deaths took place in the decade following Israel's creation. This Arab volunteer stands guard on the outskirts of Jerusalem in 1948, with rifle and grenades ready to employ.

abutted that of Egypt and Syria. The violent acts took place despite efforts by leading Western powers to prevent another major military conflict in the Middle East. In May 1950, France, Great Britain, and the United States issued a Tripartite Declaration promising to sustain the armistice agreements that had established the Green Line. The Israeli government under Prime Minister Ben-Gurion opposed that pronouncement, hoping instead to have Israel included within the anticommunist military network, the North Atlantic Treaty Organization (NATO), constructed for Western Europe, Canada, and the United States.

As for its dealings with Arab states, Israel's government adopted a policy of retaliation, to diminish the number of assaults conducted by Palestinian Arabs inside the Jewish state's borders or the Green Line. Beginning in 1952, Israel carried out military strikes against villages believed to be involved in attacks against Israelis. The next year, a new unit, headed by Colonel Ariel Sharon, was authorized to lash back at those considered to have assaulted Israel. After the murders of a Jewish woman and her two children, Sharon's men went into the Jordanian village of Qibya, where they killed more than 50 inhabitants. All the while, certain elements inside Israel, such as the *Herut* (Revisionist) Party and General Moshe Dayan, believed that Jews should control all the territory that comprised the former Palestine.

Hostility toward Israel remained pronounced in the Middle Eastern Arab states, many of which experienced social and political turmoil during the Arab-Israeli War and its aftermath. In August 1949, the Syrian army overthrew Prime Minister Khalid al-Azm, who attempted to negotiate a peace agreement with Israel; in July 1951, followers of Hajj Amin al-Husayni assassinated Jordan's King Adbullah, long the most conciliatory of Arab leaders regarding a Jewish presence in the Middle East. After the ouster of Egyptian King Farouk the following July, various young military officers appeared to desire a peaceful resolution of disputes with Israel. Nevertheless, throughout much of the Arab world, discussion abounded about destroying all vestiges of Zionist belligerence.

Particularly unsettling to Israelis in border areas along the Green Line were various acts of infiltration, which ranged from thefts to military strikes; these acts occurred in spite of the setting of mines and booby-traps, and retaliatory moves on the part of the IDF. A series of moshavim (cooperative settlements) containing Middle Eastern immigrants collapsed owing to fears of violence. A troubled Jewish Agency convinced the IDF to step up border patrols next to the Green Line. In 1954, Egyptian military operatives in Gaza, headed by Mustafa Hafiz, directed *fedayeen* ("self-sacrificers") to infiltrate Israel as retaliation for Israeli actions in the region; Jordan later employed its own fedayeen for similar purposes.

The IDF responded, after the killing of an Israeli cyclist near Rehovot. On February 28, 1955, IDF troops attacked an Egyptian military base outside Gaza, killing approximately 40. The new Egyptian strongman, Colonel Gamal Abdul Nasser, was determined to strike back. In March, Nasser ordered low-level but sustained attacks of border patrols and observation posts; Hafiz's guerrillas expanded their operations from Gaza, Jordan, and Lebanon. In response, Israel temporarily took control of Egyptian border sites along the southern Green Line, leading to a more extensive campaign of fedayeen-sparked terror in the south. Meanwhile, Israel began acquiring large shipments of arms from France; Egypt turned to the Soviets and Czechs for military assistance.

Bloody clashes, which produced considerable Egyptian and Syrian casualties, ensued in late 1955 in the Sinai, at al-Sabha and Wadi Siram, and near the Syrian border along the northeastern section of the Green Line. Then, in early April, after repeated shootings across the DMZ in Gaza and the killing of three IDF soldiers, Israeli mortars blasted into Gaza, killing 58 Egyptians and Palestinians, including 33 women and 13 children. About 200 fedayeen, packed in small units, soon poured across the border, killing nine Israeli civilians and two soldiers. Retaliating, the Israelis killed Mustafa Hafiz and his agent in Amman. From Jordan, other fedayeen, tied to the Arab legion, began conducting raids.

On July 26, 1956, Nasser, who had tightened his grip on the Straits of Tiran, nationalized the Suez Canal, providing a justification for Israeli, French, and British forces to attack Egypt. On October 21, four days after Egypt and Syria signed a military pact, representatives from the two Western European powers and Israel secretly convened in France. During the initial session,

Ben-Gurion indicated that "the elimination of Nasser" held the greatest priority but that there should also occur "the partition of Jordan, with the West Bank going to Israel and the East Bank to Iraq."[47] Under Ben-Gurion's plan, one portion of the Lebanese border, heading to the Litani River, would also end up in Israel's hands; another section would be taken over by Syria; and the remainder would be a Christian state. The Suez Canal would be internationalized, and Israel would guard the Straits of Tiran. Thus, Ben-Gurion sought to recast the arbitrary borders that ringed Israel.

At a bare minimum, Ben-Gurion hoped that Israel would be allowed to control the Sinai Peninsula, but the French insisted that the focus remain on Nasser. Following the agenda devised at the meetings, the IDF headed into the Sinai and Gaza on October 29. Two days later, the French and British demanded a truce, which would require both the Israelis and the Egyptians to pull back 10 miles from the Suez Canal. When Nasser refused, French and British planes struck Egyptian air bases, compelling Egypt to withdraw its military units from the Sinai. In early November, the Gaza Strip and Sharm al-Sheikh fell to the Israelis. On November 5, Israel and Egypt agreed to a UN demand that the fighting cease, with pressure from the United States preventing the French and British from taking over the Suez Canal. Arab states, including Egypt, drew closer to the Soviet Union, viewing it as a benefactor and arms supplier. The communist powerhouse had come to support Arab nations for two reasons: a determination to establish a foothold in the Middle East and due to the anti-Semitism that Stalin had rekindled during his final years. Israeli Prime Minister Ben-Gurion wanted IDF units to retain control of Gaza, with its 300,000 Arab inhabitants, and Sharm al-Sheikh. He agreed to withdraw Israeli forces after UN emergency forces were assigned to those regions next to the Green Line.

The results of the second Arab-Israeli War were considerable. Great Britain no longer stood as a major player in the Middle East, but Israel experienced more satisfaction, having compelled the opening of the Straits of Tiran and secured an extended period of peace along the artificial borders with Egypt and Jordan. Also, U.S. support, backed by Jewish lobbying efforts, appeared strengthened by American concerns about Soviet designs in the region. In a slap at Nasser, the United States soon proclaimed the Eisenhower Doctrine, which authorized the use of American military forces to prevent "overt armed aggression from any nation controlled by International Communism."[48] Nasser, too, notwithstanding the military pummeling Egypt had received and U.S. hostility, appeared victorious, with many Arabs viewing him as a hero who had stood up to great Western powers. His appeal resulted in the formation of the short-lived United Arab Republic (UAR), which linked Egypt and Syria. He also began talking about the desirability of another Arab-Israeli War, in which the Jewish state would be destroyed.

Once more, actions involving Israel inside the Green Line led, at least indirectly, to ferment within many of the neighboring states, this time fostered by Nasser. In July 1958, Iraqi military officers grabbed power, murdering King Faisal II and Prime Minister Nuri. Concerns about the fate of the Christian-led, pro-American regime in Lebanon subsequently led to the introduction of American marines. Worried about the stability of his government and the sanctity of Jordan's own borders, King Hussein requested the presence of British paratroopers.

Thus, as the decade neared an end, tensions remained high in the Middle East, magnified by relations between Israel and Arab nations. Hardly helping matters was the continued, festering anger regarding Israeli control of land, control many Arabs considered to be illegitimate. Even a second Arab-Israeli War had failed to resolve questions regarding the basic existence of the Jewish state, the plight of Arab refugees, and the growing determination of young Arab men to conduct guerrilla actions across the Green Line into Israel.

7

The Green Line
and the
Six-Day War

After the Suez War, a decade of incomplete peace ensued, which resulted in a strengthening of the Jewish state and a magnifying of Arab hostility regarding the Green Line and the arbitrary borders established through the 1949 armistices. Much of the Arab anger appeared to be directed by Egyptian leader Nasser and focused on the plight of Palestinian refugees. Nasser's influence throughout the Middle East remained considerable and included the sending of troops to Yemen to support an attempted coup in 1962 by young military officers who identified with him. The next year witnessed uprisings in both Iraq and Syria, which resulted in an attempt to devise a new union with Egypt, although that was soon aborted and led to yet another coup in Baghdad. During this period, many associated Nasser and his admirers with a brand of Arab nationalism that appeared far more progressive than the feudal-like monarchies of the House of Saud in Saudi Arabia and King Hussein in Jordan. Ironically, for a period, Nasser acted as a moderating force in the Arab world, such as when he sought to convince Syria not to respond militarily to Israel's diversion of water from Lake Tiberias. Nevertheless, conflicts often arose over the northern border, with Syrian and Israeli soldiers firing at one another across various demilitarized zones that abutted the Green Line.

Unhappiness with Israeli policies and the very existence of Israel continued, leading to the formation in 1964 of the Palestine Liberation Organization (PLO), which drew from *Al-Fatah*'s history; Al-Fatah had been set up in 1959 by Salah Khalaf, Khalil al-Wazir, and Yasir Arafat, among others. Arafat, whose family history remains mysterious, was supposedly related to Hajj Amin al-Husayni, and, like the other Al-Fatah founders, he studied at Cairo University but left the Egyptian metropolis after the Suez War. The PLO resided in Kuwait and, influenced by the Algerian revolutionaries who were battling against French colonialism, plotted to bring about the liberation of Palestine; particularly influential was the Algerian psychiatrist Franz Fanon, who considered revolutionary violence necessary from both a practical and a psychological vantage point.

Initially, however, the official head of the PLO was Ahmad al-Shuqayri, an attorney who had represented Saudi Arabia before the United Nations and was viewed as a Nasser lieutenant.

Historian Charles D. Smith contends that the establishment of the PLO, officially backed by the Arab League and Nasser, suggested a larger Arab commitment to the Palestinians. Nasser appeared to support the formation of the new organization to keep control of it and to prevent confrontations over the Green Line from drawing Egypt into another war. At the same time, Nasser, with little fanfare, often arrested Al-Fatah figures in both Egypt and the Gaza Strip. Jordan's King Hussein, hoping to stave off retaliatory strikes by Israel, also took Palestinian activists into custody. The PLO was intended to build on the earlier actions by fedayeen against Israel, terrorism that both Egypt and Jordan had supported.

Encouraged and generally trained by officials of the Syrian military, whose chief of staff declared, "Every soldier in our army feels that Israel must be wiped off of the map," Al-Fatah targeted Israeli sites, including water installations, as early as January 1965.[49] Following the emergence of a more radical Ba'athist regime in Syria in February 1966, that state attempted to topple Jordan's King Hussein—who sought to keep out the PLO and Al-Fatah—through Palestinian agitation. The Syrians hoped that retaliatory strikes by the IDF in the West Bank would help bring about Hussein's overthrow and convince Nasser to adopt a more radical posture. Shortly after a Syrian water diversion project was bombed by Israel on July 14, 1966, Nasser promised that he would attempt to "liberate Palestine in a revolutionary manner and not in a traditional way."[50] In early November, Egypt and Syria agreed to a mutual defense pact, a restoration of diplomatic relations, and a joint military command.

As terrorist actions, often encouraged by major Arab states, continued across the Green Line, Israel's domestic politics experienced an upheaval; those politics, in turn, were increasingly shaped by Israel's growing dependence on the United States. Aging Prime Minister Ben-Gurion, challenged by young members of his Mapai party, resigned in 1963 and, along with Moshe Dayan and Shimon Peres, formed the *Rafi* (Israeli workers') party. Menachem Begin headed the *Herut* party, which envisioned an Israel with broader borders, including the West Bank. The major Israeli parties, like the Jewish state's Arab neighbors, failed to resolve the dilemma of the Palestinian refugees, something President Kennedy was concerned about prior to his assassination in late 1963. Those parties welcomed the willingness of the United States to provide Israel with Hawk antiaircraft missiles, and the receipt of American tanks during the administration of Lyndon Baines Johnson. Both Kennedy and Johnson proved ready to deliver weapons to the Israelis as a counterweight to the massive arsenal being funneled by the Soviet Union to Arab states—particularly Egypt, Syria, and Iraq.

With the backdrop of American assistance (both military and economic), the delivery of German reparations for the Holocaust, and the presence of a skilled labor force, Israel experienced an economic boom and growing confidence. The press remained vibrant and unrestricted, the population neared 3 million, and a sense of national purpose permeated Israeli society. Historian Michael B. Oren suggests that such confidence was rooted to a large extent in faith that the IDF, which all Israelis— both men and women—were expected to join, would invariably prevail in the next "war of survival" the country would inevitably endure.

Leading Arab states, particularly Syria, were insistent that Israel be subdued, however. Previously, the Soviet Union had opposed Syrian plans to divert water from the Jordan River, calling instead for discussion focusing on partitioning. Beginning in mid-1966, the communist superpower, which had delivered $2 billion in military assistance to Arab nations since the Suez War, proved more willing to support aggressive action against Israel. Together with Syria, the Soviet Union now presented a manifesto condemning Israel as "a military arsenal and a base for aggression and blackmail against the ... Arab people"; moreover, the Soviet Union promised to support Arabs "in their just cause against colonialist Zionism."[51] Undoubtedly emboldened by Soviet backing, Syrian President Nureddin al-Atassi informed troops situated on the northern border with Israel, "We want a full-scale, popular war of liberation ... to destroy the Zionist base in Palestine."[52]

Tensions heightened in 1967, with Al-Fatah intensifying its terrorist campaign across the Green Line inside Israel and the Syrian military clashing more frequently with Israeli forces along the Golan Heights. President Nureddin al-Atassi of Syria proclaimed his support for a Palestinian war of liberation, which he likened to the wars waged by Algerians against France and by the Vietnamese against the United States. On April 7, Syrian and Israeli soldiers fired at one another along the DMZ, or the arbitrary frontier that was the DMZ in the Golan Heights, resulting in an air fight that left six Syrian MiGs downed. The next day, the Syrian government, referring to the increasing number of incidents along the Jordanian border, declared, "Our known objective is the freeing of Palestine and the liquidation of the Zionist existence there. Our army and our people will give our backing to every Arab fighter acting for the return of Palestine."[53] Such pronouncements led American policymakers to discard their earlier opposition to Israeli retaliatory strikes but also preceded a series of additional terrorist actions by Al-Fatah. By early May, guerrillas placed explosives along the Syrian and Jordanian borders and shelled northern Israel from Lebanon. Israel responded by violating demilitarized zones in crossing the Green Line, resulting in Syrian bombardments.

Increasingly, the Israeli public clamored for vengeance, demanding that Syria, not Jordan, be targeted. As rhetoric from Israeli officials intensified, President al-Atassi threatened, "Syria will launch a popular liberation war in which all the Arab masses will take part."[54] Al-Fatah conducted still more raids, moving across the Syrian and Jordanian borders that made up portions of the Green Line. Although Nasser had been restraining other Arab leaders from instigating full-scale war, many Egyptian military leaders began agitating for such a conflict, contending that

As the population and power of Israel grew, so did the tension and violence between Israel and the rest of the Middle East. In 1967, escalating tension resulted in June's Six-Day War. Here, an Israeli tank crew trains for battle.

Egypt possessed superiority over Israel in terms of planes, tanks, and weapons. In mid-May, Egypt demanded that 3,400 United Nations Emergency Force (UNEF) troops be removed from the Sinai and Gaza. Shortly thereafter, Egyptian forces replaced UNEF soldiers at Sharm al-Sheikh. Then, on May 23, the Egyptian Chief of General Staff, General `Abd al-Hakim`Amer, announced that Israeli boats would be barred from the Gulf of Eliat. Yitzhak Rabin, IDF chief of general staff, informed his generals, "It is now a question of our national survival, of to be or not to be."[55] General Aharon Yariv, director of Israeli military intelligence, insisted that Israel had to respond to the Egyptian action, which was celebrated throughout the Arab world. With Eliat threatened, Israeli Foreign Minister Abba Eban stated, "Unless a stand was made here, nobody in the Arab world ... would ever again believe in Israel's power to resist."[56]

The IDF discovered that Egypt had planned a preemptive

strike over the Green Line, although that action was evidently countermanded by Nasser following warnings by the United States and the Soviet Union. Worried that the Egyptians were planning to conduct an air strike against the Dimona nuclear plant, Israeli generals became more convinced that Israel should engage in preemptive action of its own against Egypt. Fears mounted in Israel that another Holocaust could be in the offing, with Nasser compared to Hitler. Indeed, on May 26, Nasser warned that Israel would be destroyed if war unfolded. Moshe Dayan, former IDF chief of general staff, replaced Prime Minister Levi Eshkol as defense minister. Nasser and Jordan's King Hussein inked a mutual defense accord, with an Egyptian general placed at the head of the Jordanian army. On June 3, a pair of Egyptian commando battalions flew into Jordan; the next day, a mechanized brigade from Iraq began heading toward the Jordan River. Egypt and Iraq, long hostile to one another, signed yet another defense pact. The *Voice of the Arabs* in Cairo broadcast, "The Zionist barracks in Palestine is (sic) about to collapse and be destroyed ...."[57]

Israel refrained from attacking until it appeared to receive a green light from the United States, an increasingly important ally. Initially, Israeli war planners hoped to fight only Egypt— and not on the West Bank, in Jerusalem, or along the Golan Heights, all areas boasting artificially created borders subject to dispute. Beginning shortly after 7:00 A.M. on the morning of June 5, nearly 200 Israeli planes took off, flying low to avoid Egyptian radar. By 8:00 A.M., Israeli pilots struck at Egyptian air bases, taking out nearly 200 planes—most still on the ground at the time—within 30 minutes. Another wave resulted in the destruction of additional planes, with more than 300—nearly three-quarters of the Egyptian air force—destroyed altogether. At 8:15 A.M., ground operations began, with Israeli tanks moving into Sinai. Shortly after noon, Syrian, Iraqi, and Jordanian planes joined the fight, leading to counterattacks by Israeli pilots. Yet another wave wiped out the whole Jordanian air force, two-thirds of Syria's planes, and 10 Iraqi aircraft. Thus, the first day of conflict afforded Israel almost unhampered air supremacy, allowing for effective dominion over Sinai, the West Bank, and the Golan Heights.

As warfare broke out with Jordan, Israel began to move incrementally into the West Bank, pushing at one of the Green Line's arbitrary borders. Some, including Dayan, wanted to take control of the Old City. With the fighting continuing, that possibility opened up, along with Israeli occupation of the West Bank, as the IDF swept into Bethlehem, Hebron, Jericho, and Nablus. Algerian MiGs headed for Egypt, as did Arab volunteers from North Africa. Concerned that diplomatic pressures would bring about a premature cessation of the fighting, Dayan ordered Rabin to take Gaza. A frantic retreat only heightened Egyptian difficulties in Sinai. Fearing possible Soviet intervention, Dayan wanted to avoid war on the northern front, but with both Egypt and Jordan subdued, the Israeli defense minister supported a move past the Green Line and into the Golan Heights. That feat was accomplished shortly after a cease-fire became effective on June 10.

When the Six-Day War ended, Egypt had suffered the death of at least 10,000 soldiers, with another 5,000 missing; Jordan experienced 700 casualties and Syria 450. Israel saw about 800 of its soldiers perish, with another 2,600 or so wounded. Fifteen Israeli soldiers were prisoners of war, in contrast to 5,000 Egyptians, 550 Jordanians, and 365 Syrians. Altogether, 200,000 to 300,000 Arabs scattered from the West Bank and Gaza, many ending up on Jordan's East Bank. In addition, 80,000 to 90,000 Arabs departed from the Golan Heights, heightening the problem of Palestinian refugees.

Altered territorial holdings clearly demonstrated how artificial the entire process of establishing borders in the area had been. Israel now controlled a much larger amount of territory than was envisioned under the armistice agreements of 1949 that established the Green Line. That included the Egyptian Sinai all the way to the Gulf of Suez, the Gaza Strip, the West Bank, and the Syrian Golan. The Six-Day War resulted in Israel taking over 42,000 square miles of land, enabling the Jewish state to emerge out of the ashes almost four times larger than when Ben-Gurion had issued his declaration of independence. Israel now possessed full control of the Holy City and religious sites

UN RESOLUTION 242

On November 22, 1967, the United Nations passed Resolution 242, which provided the basis for a political resolution of the conflicts pertaining to the Green Line and the existence of arbitrary borders shaping Israel. The measure called for Israel to withdraw "from territories" it had occupied since the Six-Day War. It also insisted on "termination of all claims or states of belligerency and respect for and acknowledgement of the sovereignty, territorial integrity and political independence of every State in the area." Resolution 242 affirmed the right of freedom of navigation through waterways in the region and a "just settlement of the refugee problem."*

The wording of Resolution 242 produced debates regarding the intentions of its designers. Although some contended that Israel was compelled to depart from the Sinai, the Gaza Strip, the West Bank, the Golan Heights, and East Jerusalem, others contested that notion. Both Arthur Goldberg and Lord Caradon, the ambassadors to the United Nations from the United States and Great Britain, respectively, when Resolution 242 was passed, later declared that it did not require Israel to return to pre-1967 borders. As Caradon acknowledged, Israel's situation prior to the Six-Day War was "undesirable and artificial," being determined by the old armistice lines alone.** The resolution also failed to halt belligerent acts, with strikes into Israel or Israeli-occupied territories continuing and Arab states long refusing to recognize the Jewish state's right to exist. The refugee question remained complicated and unsettled; it involved both Palestinian Arabs and Middle Eastern Jews (700,000 in all) who had been forced to depart from their homes. No financial compensation was allocated for property confiscated from either Arabs or Jews. All of this illuminated the difficulties related to the drawing of arbitrary borders in the Middle East.

---

*Quoted in "U. N. Security Council Resolution 242," *Middle East Historical Documents*, http://www.mideast-web.org/242.htm. Online.

**Quoted in Joseph Telushkin, *Jewish Literacy: The Most Important Things to Know About the Jewish Religion, Its People, and Its History*. New York: William Morrow, 1991, p. 316.

sacred to three major religions. All this led Arabs to refer to the Six-Day War as "The Setback" or "The Disaster."[58]

These facts, coupled with the plight of the refugees and the stunning defeat suffered by Egypt, Syria, and Jordan, resulted in attacks on Jewish neighborhoods across portions of North Africa and the Middle East. Of Arab leaders, only Tunisian president Habib Bourguiba and Morocco's King Hassan condemned the assaults on Jews, their homes, and synagogues. Thousands of Jews faced expulsion, which generally also involved the loss of property. Israel, which now held sway over 1.2 million Palestinians within greatly expanded borders, soon established military administration over both the West Bank and Gaza but generally allowed Palestinian religious and secular leaders to retain the positions they had occupied before the war. A less tolerant approach involved the removal of poor homes in the Mughrabi neighborhood of Jerusalem near the Western Wall and the obliteration of three Arab villages in the Latrun corridor. The Six-Day War, which resulted in the pushing back of the Green Line, altered the balance of power in the Middle East for quite some time. The Arab states, particularly Egypt, Syria, and Jordan, suffered crushing defeats and the loss of considerable amounts of territory. Israel, thanks to its stunning victory, acquired control over a vastly greater landscape, which seemingly afforded it greater protection from hostile neighbors. Once more, however, the acquisition of additional land resulted in Israeli responsibility for vast numbers of Arab residents, many of whom remained hostile to the Jewish state. As events bore out, the construction of new artificial boundaries provided seeds for greater hatred, more hostilities, and ultimately, questions regarding how Israel could remain democratic while serving as an occupying force.

8

The War of Attrition and the October War

Shortly after the conclusion of the Six-Day War, Israel's Foreign Minister Abba Eban informed Israeli diplomats, "There is a new reality and it points at talks on peace and security. Those aspects, it must be emphasized, have a territorial dimension. The world and Arab world must know that there's no turning back the clock to 1957 or 1948." Still, he underscored, "everything is fluid, flexible, and open."[59] Labor Minister Yigal Allon, seeking to expand his nation's borders beyond the Green Line, called for Israel to rebuild and settle in the Old City's Jewish Quarter and to ring East Jerusalem with new Jewish neighborhoods. Indeed, Allon, like Defense Minister Moshe Dayan, urged that Arabs be removed from the Jewish Quarter; some 300 families soon were.

On June 19, 1967, the Israeli cabinet, meeting at Mount Scopus, discussed the explosive issue of the Jewish state's expanded borders. Cabinet members agreed that the Egyptian Sinai and the Syrian Golan Heights should be swapped in order to maintain peace but demanded that certain sections be demilitarized and the Straits of Tiran opened to Israeli ships. That message was soon conveyed to the U.S. government, which in turn relayed it to Cairo and Damascus, where the proposal was summarily rejected. The Israeli cabinet members had failed to mention the Gaza Strip, a 363-kilometer plot of land, and had made no determination about the West Bank, which included East Jerusalem. Top Israeli political figures did appear to agree that there would be no complete return to the pre-1967 borders or the Green Line. Some believed that Israel should annex both Gaza and the West Bank, historic sites for *Eratz Israel* (the land of Israel), with Menachem Begin contending, "The concept of autonomy ... will lead to a Palestinian State."[60] Labor Minister Allon also opposed the June 19 resolution, arguing instead that Israeli settlements be established in the West Bank. These would help establish a defense belt, distinguishing "an agreed, independent Arab State, surrounded by Israeli territory."[61]

In late June, Israel officially annexed East Jerusalem and surrounding portions of the West Bank and knocked down concrete walls that had splintered the city. In July, Allon proposed a territorial compromise that would split control of the West Bank between Israel and Jordan. Israel would retain a six- or seven-mile security strip beyond the Green Line along the Jordan River valley, to stave off an Arab invasion. With the exception of additional slender border strips, Jordan would possess control over the rest of the West Bank.

As Israeli government leaders argued about the fate of the West Bank and other occupied territories, movements arose demanding the retention from those lands outside the Green Line. The advocates of retaining the gains from the Six-Day War ranged from the largely secular Land of Israel Movement to religious nationalists, who saw divine inspiration as compelling the expansion of Israel's borders. The religious nationalists headed into the West Bank territories they called Judea and Samaria to establish settlements that would help usher in a greater Israel. They considered Israeli control of Judea and Samaria to be divinely inspired, part of biblical Israel.

Two other settlements, supported by the IDF, appeared in the Golan Heights and the Sinai. After the Israeli cabinet allowed fields in the Golan Heights to be cultivated, Dayan, Allon, and another cabinet minister backed the building of a series of outposts in the north. In September, the cabinet received news that a settlement was being constructed between Bethlehem and Hebron, near where Kfar Etzion had existed before it was destroyed by the Arab legion during the 1948–1949 Arab-Israeli War. In early 1968, cabinet ministers agreed to the establishment of a pair of settlements in the southern Jordan Valley. Other settlements, again beyond the Green Line, soon appeared in the Golan Heights, the Gaza Strip, and the West Bank.

Israeli government forces continued to have contrasting views regarding the settlement movement that insisted on expanding the nation's borders; some opposed it altogether, others offered qualified support, and still others championed it unreservedly. Ultimately, the government allowed the IDF to protect the settlers while providing necessary water supplies and electricity. Benny Morris argues that the government's land policy proved most crucial, however, with Israel expropriating all the land in the territories and joining with settler groups to purchase other tracts or take over uncultivated plots beyond the Green Line. By 1973, Israel had set up 17 settlements in the West Bank alone, along with 7 in the Gaza Strip and the Sinai Peninsula's northwestern sector, 3 in Sinai, and 19 in the Golan Heights. By that date, Labor party (which emerged from the Mapai party through a new coalition in 1968) leaders like Dayan championed the right of individuals to purchase land in the West Bank.

The settlements and Israeli control of the occupied territories beyond the Green Line produced an ironic result. After the Six-Day War, Israel contained within its borders more Palestinians than any another nation—some 1.5 million, including 1.1 million in the lands acquired in June 1967. Of 600,000 Palestinians in the West Bank, 60,000 resided in refugee camps, while in Gaza, 170,000 of 210,000 Palestinians did so. Moreover, the war, which had proven so catastrophic to the Palestinians and so devastating to Arab nations, served to catalyze a sense of Palestinian identity and the demand for nationhood. The cementing of Israeli military control only heightened frustration and anger within the Palestinian community, notwithstanding Dayan's implementation of an open bridges policy. That approach allowed Palestinians on the West Bank to establish economic ties with those residing on the East Bank. Dayan also pushed for open access to Jerusalem's holy sites, including the Temple Mount in the Old City, and to the Tomb of the Patriarchs in Hebron. Nevertheless, Palestinian leaders were enraged that Dayan and the Israeli government refused to grant them autonomy in the West Bank; at this stage, Labor party leaders, like those in more conservative political organizations, opposed the idea of Palestinian nationhood.

Dayan and other Israeli military officials helped institute other policies that infuriated the Palestinians. Dayan supported the unification of Jerusalem, which resulted in the annexation of

East Jerusalem. He backed Israel's retention of the West Bank and the integration of the economies of both the West Bank and the Gaza Strip with the Jewish state. Dayan favored a policy of transferring Arab inhabitants of the occupied territories out of the landscape had made up Palestine prior to the 1948–1949 Arab-Israeli War. After the Six-Day War, Dayan informed senior military officers that Arab emigration should not be discouraged, "because after all, we want to create a new map" with reshaped borders now possible because of military conquest.[62] Protests ensued on the West Bank, leading to attempted strikes and demonstrations that produced Israeli crackdowns. Al-Fatah, led by Yasir Arafat, was initially unable to convince Palestinians to support a mass movement to resist Israeli occupation. Instead, Palestinians soon resorted to armed resistance, tossing grenades at IDF forces and placing bombs in Israeli cities. Israelis required Palestinians to carry identity cards, to obtain permits for travel, and to undergo body searches and roadblocks in restricted areas, further fueling the rage that induced a growing number of young men to directly oppose the occupation.

More than at any point since the 1948–1949 Arab-Israeli War, Arab states in the Middle East now began to pay greater attention to the plight of the Palestinians; the Arab nations that had lost territory during the most recent conflict also demanded return of those lands on the other side of the Green Line. King Hussein hoped to receive promises from the United States that the West Bank would be returned to Jordan and its military rebuilt. Syria refused any efforts to resolve disputes diplomatically. Nasser sought to adopt both a diplomatic stance and a threat of additional military action. During a meeting in Sudan in late August, which Syria refused to attend, Arab leaders "agreed to unite their political efforts at the international and diplomatic level" to bring about the "withdrawal of the aggressive Israeli forces from the Arabs lands" recently occupied. They refused to discard previously held principles, "namely no peace with Israel, no recognition of Israel, no negotiations with it, and insistence on the rights of the Palestinian people in their own country."[63]

With a stalemate in place, the United Nations met in late November, when it issued Resolution 242, which was the by-product of a compromise between the United States, the Soviet Union, and various allies on both sides. Although the measure underscored "the inadmissibility of the acquisition of territory by war," it insisted on "a just and lasting peace," calling, in effect, for land outside the Green Line to be traded for peace. Israel was urged to withdraw "from territories occupied" during the Six-Day War, and the Arabs were instructed to halt belligerent actions and to recognize the sovereignty and "territorial integrity" of each state in the region. The UN Security Council also acknowledged that the "refugee problem" had to be resolved.[64]

Because both Arafat and Jordan's King Hussein were worried that Israel intended to annex the West Bank, they formed an uneasy alliance to prevent this. Hussein operated through diplomatic channels, reaching out to the United States and speaking privately with Israeli officials, but he refused the open negotiations the Israelis demanded. Consequently, Hussein allowed Al-Fatah to conduct operations across the Green Line against Israel but found it difficult to control the guerrilla group, which began to dominate Jordanian refugee camps. In December 1967, a competitor for Al-Fatah emerged: the Popular Front for the Liberation of Palestine (PFLP), headed by Dr. George Habash, a Christian who envisioned a large-scale Arab revolutionary movement capable of radicalizing Arab regimes. In 1968, various groups associated with the PFLP employed Lebanon as a staging ground for the hijacking of airplanes. By the close of the following year, Israel encountered PLO raids along the borders with Lebanon and Jordan. That same year also witnessed an escalation in guerrilla strikes on the Gaza Strip.

Beginning in early 1971, the PLO responded to the stalemate and its ouster from Jordan by conducting a series of terrorist strikes, relying on its Black September faction. In May 1972, a Sabena plane bound for Tel Aviv was hijacked at Lydda Airport, with an ensuing demand for the release of hundreds of jailed

Palestinian guerrillas. In the midst of negotiations, Israeli forces freed the passengers and crew, with two terrorists and one passenger dying in the process. Additional operations by the PFLP produced more casualties. Then, in September 1972, in the midst of the Olympic Games in Munich, Black September terrorists murdered 11 Israeli athletes and coaches. The IDF struck at PLO bases but also ordered the *Mossad*, the Israeli intelligence agency, to assassinate any Black September and PFLP leaders they could find.

During the same period, relations between Israel and Egypt also proved strained, with a war of attrition taking place across the latest arbitrary borders that had been shaped. Both countries continued to build up their military forces in the wake of the Six-Day War. Pressured by the Soviet Union, Egypt accepted UN Resolution 242 but refused to formally recognize Israel, which in turn demanded direct negotiations that Egypt found unacceptable. By 1968, Nasser opted for a policy of military confrontation to bring about a change in relations with its Jewish neighbor, although a series of clashes occurred shortly after the 1967 war. Egypt employed artillery to target IDF forces along the Suez Canal and supported various commando strikes over the Green Line into Israel. In response, the Israelis began constructing the Bar-Lev Line, a series of 35 forts along the Suez, believed to be capable of withstanding any assault from Egypt. The IDF also conducted raids into Egypt, striking at the northern infrastructure. Nasser failed to back down, notwithstanding a sustained aerial offensive that wiped out Egypt's air defense system and a tank assault that pushed Egyptian forces back 50 miles.

The conflict continued as the Soviet Union and the United States sought to bring about a cease-fire. In December 1969, U.S. Secretary of State William Rogers called for Israel to return to its pre-1967 borders on the Green Line, in return for each side's recognition of the other's sovereignty, albeit through informal negotiations. New Israeli air strikes occurred that may have been designed to bring about Nasser's ouster. These proved counterproductive because Moscow agreed to provide Egypt with new advanced missiles, along with Soviet MiGs and pilots. Secretary of State Rogers urged all parties to rely on UN Resolution 242 to conduct negotiations, and called on Israel to withdraw from the territories occupied beyond the Green Line since the Six-Day War. Israel accepted only after being informed that the Nixon administration would not support a pullback to the pre-1967 level. A cease-fire occurred in August 1970 following the death of 367 Israelis and perhaps as many as 10,000 Egyptians.

A series of events transpired later that year that altered events in the Middle East. In late September, Nasser died of a massive heart attack and was replaced as Egyptian head of state by Anwar Sadat. That same month, Hussein's army attacked PLO forces in Amman, the beginning of a lengthy campaign that eventually led to the organization's departure from Jordan. In November 1970, the PLO acquired a new ally when Hafiz Assad assumed the presidency of Syria. UN Ambassador Gunnar Jarring continued his efforts to mediate disputes in the Middle East, relying on Resolution 242. Eventually, Jarring sought to convince Israel to return to its pre-1967 borders in return for the effective demilitarization of the Sinai and the placement of UN troops at Sharm al-Sheikh; Egypt was also to allow passage through the Suez Canal. Agreeing to these provisions, Sadat insisted that the refugee dilemma be resolved. Israel refused to accept Sadat's demand and proved unwilling to withdraw to the prewar borders on the Green Line. Once again, Israel demanded that direct negotiations take place, without any conditions.

By early 1971, Egyptian president Sadat evidently decided that war was unavoidable. He signed an agreement with the Soviet Union that required the communist superpower to assist Egypt in a military campaign. In June, Sadat declared his readiness "to sacrifice a million Egyptian soldiers" to win back the territory lost during the Six-Day War.[65] Distressed by the Soviets' opposition to war and hoping to win favor with the United States, Sadat, in July 1972, kicked thousands of military advisers from the Soviet Union out of Egypt. Both Israel and the United States decided that Egypt was now more vulnerable militarily and less inclined to warfare. In fact, Sadat continued to plan for hostilities, evidently obtaining, during a meeting in Egypt in April 1973, Assad's agreement to fight Israel.

Israel, for its part, exuded overconfidence, with Defense Minister Dayan suggesting that war would not be likely break out for a full decade. On October 6, however, in the afternoon of *Yom Kippur*, the holiest day in the Jewish year—as well as the anniversary of Muhammad's triumph over Meccan foes at Badr—Egyptian and Syrian soldiers assaulted IDF forces. The fabled Israeli intelligence operatives had failed to anticipate the war, arguing against the likelihood of its unfolding; not helping matters was the deception by a highly placed Egyptian official, whom the Mossad, and hence the Israeli government, had come to rely on heavily since he first provided information during the War of Attrition. Most Israeli political and military leaders remained untroubled, despite Egyptian and Syrian troop movements to the Green Line or the borders of lands taken by Israel during the Six-Day War. The Israelis also failed to heed the warnings of King Hussein, who, in a secret session in Tel Aviv with Prime Minister Golda Meir, insisted that war appeared imminent. Thus, the Israeli public was stunned as the Arabs achieved initial successes that resulted in Egyptian advances across the Suez into Sinai and Syrian advances across the Purple Line, the cease-fire point in the Golan Heights following the Six-Day War. Relying on antiaircraft artillery, tanks, and fighter planes, Egyptian units shot down a series of Israeli planes, overran IDF bases, and pummeled scores of Israeli tanks. In the South, Egyptian soldiers, who greatly outnumbered their foes, battered the forts along the Bar-Levi Line intended to provide an impregnable defense in the Sinai. On the third day of fighting, the IDF finally conducted its first coordinated counteroffensive in the Sinai, but it too proved to be a debacle.

Up north, as Syrian tanks rolled across the Purple Line toward the Jordan Valley, Dayan warned that unless the enemy advance was halted, "This is the destruction of the Third Temple"; he urged a pullback from the territories.[66] On the morning of October 8, Israel undertook a successful counterattack. Israeli forces in the Golan Heights, which had come close to collapsing, began encircling Syrian units, pummelling them from the air and destroying hundreds of Syrian tanks and other armored vehicles. Although the battle for Mount Hermon continued, the Israeli and Syrian armies returned to their prewar Purple Line positions by October 10. Meanwhile, Israeli planes strafed Syria, knocking out most of its airfields, blasting the Syrian command centers in Damascus, and destroying power stations and oil storage depots. Nevertheless, grueling fighting continued over the old borders as Israeli forces advanced 20 miles south of Damascus. By October 14, most of the IDF's firepower was redirected to the southern front, although Mount Hermon was recaptured several days later.

The war in the south continued to go badly for the Israelis until Egypt conducted a second offensive on October 14, which was intended to alleviate pressure on Syrian forces in the Golan Heights. Conducting a series of thrusts over a 100-mile front, the Egyptians attacked, eventually suffering the loss of hundreds of tanks in the face of IDF fighter-bombers and tanks. The Israelis subsequently carried out their own counteroffensive on October 16, which eventually resulted in a crossing of the Suez Canal and the IDF's retaking of territory lost earlier in the war. Then, on October 22, a Soviet-American–brokered cease-fire took effect. Both sides soon violated it, however, with the Israelis capturing 4,500 Egyptian soldiers.

By October 27, UN observers arrived at the front lines. The October, or Yom Kippur, War resulted in approximately 2,300 Israeli fatalities, along with 5,500 injuries and 294 captivities. Egypt suffered 12,000 fatalities, with 35,000 wounded and 8,400 taken prisoner. Syria experienced about 3,000 fatalities, with 5,600 wounded and 411 captured; these included a small number of Iraqis and Moroccans. Material losses were considerable too, with Israel losing 102 planes and 400 tanks; Egypt, losing 235 planes and 1,000 tanks; and Syria, losing 135 planes and 1,150 tanks. Egypt also suffered the loss of

Conflict over Israel's border erupted into war again in 1973. In this photograph, an Israeli soldier flies the Star of David over the recaptured east bank of the Suez Canal. The Yom Kippur, or October, War resulted in thousands of casualties, but produced no drastic changes to the existing border.

scores of surface-to-air missile (SAM) batteries with Israel losing but one.

Unlike previous Arab-Israeli conflicts, the October, or Yom Kippur, War resulted in no dramatic alteration of existing borders. Israel did acquire an additional 500 square kilometers in the north, which included the Syrian side of Mount Hermon and Tel Shams, and 1,600 square kilometers along the Suez Canal's west bank; Egypt actually retook two territorial strips, some six miles in depth, in the Sinai. Israel failed to win another sweeping victory like the ones attained during the 1948–1949, 1956, and 1967 wars, however. At the same time, Israel more than held on to the territory it had acquired beyond the Green

Line during the Six-Day War. Consequently, Arabs and Israelis appeared to draw different lessons from this latest conflict, which had involved a determined effort to recapture lost territory and thereby recast Israel's arbitrary borders. Arabs believed that they had come close to toppling the previously invincible Jewish state, and the Israelis recognized how close to a disaster the October War had been. Israel's foes thought that they had restored their own honor, supposedly lost in the 1967 debacle, and Israelis were enraged by the political and military blunders of their leaders.

9

Camp David,
Lebanon, and
the Intifada

The October, or Yom Kippur, War produced a crisis of confidence in Israel but also afforded unprecedented opportunities for peaceful negotiations regarding the arbitrary borders that a series of martial encounters had produced. After the war, the performances of Israeli Prime Minister Meir and Defense Minister Dayan were condemned. Although the Labor party won the national elections in December 1973, its hold on power was weakened, and a new right-of-center party, *Likud*, emerged, led by Menachem Begin and Ariel Sharon. In April, with criticism continuing and protest movements surging, both Meir and Dayan resigned, and a new government was formed by Yitzhak Rabin, who had served as chief of staff during the Six-Day War and later as his nation's ambassador to the United States.

With U.S. Secretary of State Henry Kissinger engaging in shuttle diplomacy, Egypt and Israel signed an accord on January 18, 1974, which led to the withdrawal of Israeli forces from the west bank of the Suez Canal. In contrast to the Egyptians, the Syrians proved unwilling to negotiate directly with Israeli representatives, instead reverting to a small war of attrition involving the Bashan enclave and battling with Israeli forces over the Syrian Hermon. After the signing of an agreement in Geneva in late May 1974, the IDF did remove its troops from the Bashan, the Syrian Hermon, and a small amount of territory located west of the Purple Line, which was to be patrolled by 1,250 UN forces.

Still unresolved was the matter of Israeli occupation of the Gaza Strip, the West Bank, and much of the Sinai Peninsula and the Golan Heights, all situated outside the Green Line. In September 1975, Rabin agreed to a second pact with Egypt that resulted in IDF forces moving beyond the strategic passes and Egypt's acquiring of access to various oil fields in the Gulf of Suez. Both sides agreed "not to resort to the threat of use of forces or military blockade against each other" and to resolve disputes peacefully. Additionally, they promised to attain "a final and just peace settlement" based on UN Resolution 338, issued during the October War.[67] By contrast, Israel refused to pull back from the West Bank, allowing instead for additional settlements, as encouraged by the *Gush Emunim* movement. This further discredited King Hussein in the eyes of many Palestinians. Arab leaders, meeting in Rabat, Morocco, in October 1974, proclaimed "the right of the Palestinian people to establish an independent national authority under the command of the Palestinian Liberation Organization"; the delegates deemed the PLO the "sole legitimate representative of the Palestinian people, in any Palestinian territory that is liberated."[68]

Although the Labor party had increasingly supported settlements on the West Bank, Israeli voters in May 1977 elected the Likud party, headed by Begin. Previously adverse to the idea of trading land for peace, Begin came to accept UN Resolution 242 as the basis for talks with Egypt. Encouraged by the U.S. administration of Jimmy Carter and the Soviet Union's regime under Leonid Brezhnev, the governments of Begin and Egypt's Anwar Sadat conducted the Camp David talks, which involved extensive negotiations to achieve acceptance of the arbitrary borders that characterized the Middle East. In March 1979, after Sadat made a historic visit to Jerusalem, the Egyptians and Israelis signed a "framework," with the Israelis undertaking a pullback from the Sinai (most of which was to be demilitarized) and Egypt agreeing to recognize the state of Israel. Israel was afforded unrestricted movement through the Suez Canal, the Gulf of Suez, the Straits of Tiran, and the Gulf of Aqaba. UN forces were stationed in the Rafa approaches and at Sharm al-Sheikh. According to a "Framework for Peace," representatives from Jordan and the Palestinians, along with Egyptian and Israeli negotiators, were supposed to bring about the "peaceful and orderly transfer of authority" and movement toward "full autonomy" in the West Bank and Gaza.[69]

As relations between Israel and Egypt normalized, Israeli settlers in the occupied territories beyond the Green Line resisted, often resulting in government efforts to appease them, adding another wrinkle to the issue of arbitrary borders. At the same time, discussion regarding autonomy for Gaza and the West Bank foundered badly, in part because Begin had no intention of

Egyptian President Anwar Sadat, left, U.S. President Jimmy Carter, center, and Israeli Prime Minister Menachem Begin, are seen here after signing the 1979 peace treaty between Egypt and Israel. President Carter gathered the leaders at Camp David to conduct negotiations that successfully resulted in peace between the Arabs and Jews.

granting Arabs self-rule in those regions. Indeed, by 1981, 70 settlements outside Israel's official borders were in place, with some 16,000 inhabitants, a development encouraged by Begin and Agriculture Minister Ariel Sharon. Sadat experienced opposition of his own, being vilified by much of the Arab world and particularly by Muslim fundamentalists, many of whom viewed favorably the revolutionary regime of Iran's Ayatollah Khomeini. On October 6, 1981, radical fundamentalists murdered Sadat, but his successor, Hosni Mubarak, adhered to the Camp David agreements. A month later, Begin moved to strengthen Israeli control of the West Bank by seeking to establish a Palestinian governing authority beholden to Israel. The Israeli chief of staff, General Rafael Eitan, also employed an iron-fist approach regarding growing Palestinian resistance on the West Bank.

With its southern border protected and the West Bank apparently pacified, the Israeli government decided to strike at the

PLO, now situated above Israel's northern border in Lebanon. Zionists had wanted southern Lebanon to be part of a Jewish state in the aftermath of World War I and later worried that Muslims would dominate that area. Zionists envisioned an alliance with Lebanese Christians, the Maronites, who were outnumbered by Muslims in Lebanon. In the midst of the 1948–1949 Arab-Israeli War, Israeli leaders had hoped that Maronites would take power and sign a peace treaty with Israel. During the 1950s, both Ben-Gurion and Chief of the General Staff Dayan considered sending the IDF into Lebanon to set up a friendly Christian government. Lebanon avoided participation in the Six-Day War, although PLO guerrillas subsequently conducted raids over the Green Line along the Lebanese border into Israel. Such raids greatly increased in the 1970s, but the IDF largely cut off Palestinian incursions by the middle of the decade. The beginning of civil war in Lebanon in April 1975 also crippled the guerrillas, who suffered a number of severe setbacks.

The PLO began to consolidate its control over southern Lebanon and refugee camps located near Beirut and Tripoli. As Benny Morris suggested, the PLO amounted to a "state-within-a-state," with its own army, taxes, police, courts, schools, and medical care.[70] The PLO also continued to conduct raids across the border into Israel, which resulted in IDF counterstrikes. By March 1978, the Israelis carved out a type of security zone—dominated by Christians—that provided six miles of protection to the border. Additionally, UN forces soon arrived as part of a plan to remove Israeli forces and further demilitarize the area. Nevertheless, the PLO continued to rain artillery and rocket fire on Israel or to carry out raids, and the Israelis responded in kind.

In 1981, after an exchange of rocket and artillery fire and assaults by Israeli planes, the IDF undertook attacks on PLO buildings in Beirut, which resulted in hundreds of civilian casualties. As the PLO kept firing rockets and shells over the arbitrarily drawn northern border, thousands of Israeli settlers fled southward. Following an American-sponsored cease-fire,

which was frequently violated, Begin and his new defense minister, Ariel Sharon, decided to remove the PLO from Lebanon.
They also wanted to ensure Christian dominance of Lebanon
and the ouster of the Syrian army from that country. In early
June 1982, Israeli jets bombed West Beirut, resulting in the PLO's
shelling of northern Israel.

Sharon then initiated his plan, Big Pines, which called for
striking 25 miles above the Green Line into Lebanon, to remove
the PLO from that country's southern sector. Eventually, Israeli
and Syrian forces battled one another, and the possibility of a
larger conflict arose. The Syrians suffered terrible losses, including the destruction of their air defense system and the downing
of two dozen MiGs and top pilots. The war splintered Lebanon
further, between Israeli-, Syrian-, and Christian-held areas. The
IDF moved all the way to Beirut and the Damascus road, and
Beirut was divided between Christian, Syrian, and PLO strongholds. The Israelis undertook a siege of Beirut that lasted over
two months and involved artillery and aerial strikes; food, fuel,
and water shortages in the city; and growing numbers of civilian
casualties. The Israeli military experienced dissension, but Arab
states hardly protested. Still, Israel's image suffered as televised
reports unveiled something of the war's destructive path.
Nevertheless, the PLO evacuated Lebanon in late August, scat-
tering into several nearby countries with leaders moving to
Tunisia. Then, shortly after the assassination of Bashir Gemayel,
the top Lebanese Maronite politician and an ally of Israel,
Phalangist militia forces headed into the Sabra and Shatila
refugee camps. Aided by Israeli illumination rounds, the
Phalangists killed 450 to 800 individuals, many of them male
Palestinians. Israel's own Kahan Commission later declared the
IDF to have been complicit in the massacre.

Israel gradually withdrew from Lebanon in the midst of
heightened guerrilla activity against the IDF, starting in October
1982. After the departure of Palestinian forces, the guerrillas
tended to be associated with the Iranian-sponsored Shi'i militia,
the *Hizbollah*, particularly the faction known as *Islamic Jihad*.

Members of the Iranian Revolutionary Guards and Syrian intelligence agents assisted the Hizbollah, as did some Palestinians. By June 1985, Israeli forces withdrew to the security zone, previously dominated by Maronite Christians. During the previous three years, Israel had experienced 650 fatalities along with 3,000 wounded through its operations in Lebanon; the PLO had lost 1,000 individuals and the Syrians between 500 and 1,000. Civilian casualties were high as well. After the Israeli pullback, terrorist strikes, including suicide bombings, continued in an effort to drive the IDF out of Lebanon.

Israel's Lebanese venture did result in the decimation of the PLO military apparatus north of the Israeli border and the general departure of the PLO from Lebanon. The PLO had not suffered a mortal blow in the fashion envisioned by both Begin and Sharon, however. Israel had also badly weakened the Syrian air defense system, but President Assad's hold on power was hardly lessened. Most striking of all, the removal of the PLO had not produced a diminution of the threat across the northern arbitrary border; instead, the even deadlier Hizbollah now attacked Israeli forces in the security zone, and eventually another war of attrition began, this time initiated by Hizbollah. Finally, Syrian dominance in Lebanon became far more pronounced, notwithstanding military setbacks suffered at the hands of the IDF.

With Israel preoccupied about its northern border with Lebanon, a popular uprising, the *Intifada*, emerged on the West Bank after the crashing of an Israeli tank-transport that killed four Palestinians and injured others in Gaza on December 8, 1987. This eruption represented frustration regarding both Israeli and established Palestinian leaders. It occurred after years of relative economic prosperity in the wake of the Six-Day War. For the first 10 years after the conflict, improved wages and the allowance of a measure of self-rule, coupled with the relatively slow growth of Jewish settlements, appeared to placate the majority of Palestinians on the West Bank. After Begin assumed the prime ministership of Israel in 1978, that changed, with the number of settlements outside the Green Line increasing nearly tenfold through 1987. Moreover, the newest settlements, in contrast to earlier ones, tended to be situated close to Arab communities and resulted in a confiscation of Arab land. Anger heightened when Defense Minister Sharon and Chief of Staff Rafael Eitan employed an iron-fist policy to destroy Palestinian resistance and to redistribute Arab land to Jewish settlers. When demonstrations increased, starting in 1985, along with a cycle of violence and counterviolence, the Israelis arrested greater numbers of Arabs and resorted to a policy employed by the British during the 1930s: the destruction of the dwelling places of those accused of politically motivated violent acts.

Violence also escalated in Gaza, where water restrictions were initiated to benefit some 2,500 settlers in 16 settlements, notwithstanding resulting economic difficulties for 750,000 Palestinians. Still, the annual per capita income in Gaza mushroomed twenty-fold during the first 15 years of occupation. Nevertheless, armed resistance had cropped up soon after the Israeli takeover in 1967, lengthening four years later when the IDF carried out various deportations. A decade later, violence reemerged after an Israeli-controlled civilian administration was instituted in both Gaza and the West Bank. By the mid-1980s, Islamic militancy appeared in Gaza through *al-Jihad*, which was derived from the Muslim Brotherhood and encouraged armed resistance against the IDF to bring about liberation. As on the West Bank, violence in Gaza, which possessed one of the world's densest population, and where harder economic times had taken hold, now intensified.

Beginning in Gaza on December 8, 1987, the Intifada unfolded in a largely spontaneous fashion, to the astonishment of both the Israelis and the PLO, still weakened after its ouster from Lebanon. For the most part, those participating in the Intifada were young and poor, and they chose to rely on demonstrations and rock-throwing, initially prohibiting the use of guns and knives. By January 1988, leaders throughout the territories were urging the establishment of an independent Palestinian nation, guided by the PLO, that would accept Israel's right to exist. The PLO and a new organization, *Hamas* or the Islamic Resistance Movement, sought to spearhead the ongoing Intifada. Derived from the Muslim Brotherhood, Hamas favored the formation of a Palestinian state based on religious ideas; similar to Islamic Jihad, it opposed the possibility of compromise that Arafat appeared to be offering.

Israeli government officials from a Likud-Labor national unity government led by Yitzhak Shamir and Shimon Peres, including Defense Minister Yitzhak Rabin, denied that the Intifada involved political protest, terming it terrorism. Members

YASIR ARAFAT

Although mystery surrounds his early years, Yasir Arafat was born in August 1929, in either Jerusalem or Cairo, to a prominent family known for its anti-Zionist beliefs. After the death of his mother when he was a young child, Arafat resided in Jerusalem, where he became concerned about Palestine's future. As a student at Cairo University, he ran guns into Palestine during the 1948–1949 Arab-Israeli War. Soon after obtaining a degree in architectural engineering, Arafat helped establish Al-Fatah, a guerrilla organization influenced by Nasser that called for terrorist strikes into Israel. After serving in the Egyptian army during the Suez War, Arafat moved to Kuwait, where he worked as an engineer and trained commandos.

After the Six-Day War, more Arab leaders proved receptive to Arafat's insistence that guerrilla action be undertaken against Israel. In 1969, the PLO incorporated Arafat's fedayeen, and he was selected as PLO chairman. Within a short while, he headed the Palestinian Revolution Forces. Increasingly, the PLO, under Arafat's guidance, discarded its previous pan-Arabist orientation, focusing instead on the quandary of the Palestinians. In 1970, King Hussein, who was worried that the PLO threatened his rule, forced Arafat and his guerrillas out of Jordan. Nevertheless, the PLO intensified the scope of its terrorist actions, highjacking airliners, attacking Israeli civilians, and murdering 11 Israeli athletes and coaches during the 1972 Olympic Games in Munich. The next year, Arafat served as the PLO's military commander. In 1974, the Arab League declared the PLO to be the lone authentic representative of the Palestinians.

of the IDF demanded curfews, shot at demonstrators, beat prisoners, liberally employed tear gas, and vandalized houses situated close to demonstration sites. Five weeks after the Intifada began, the Israelis had killed 33 Palestinians while suffering no fatalities of their own and had imprisoned nearly 2,000. Israel also resorted to assassination, killing Khalil al-Wazir, who was considered to be guiding the Intifada. Rather than quelling the uprising, however, Israeli actions only strengthened the determination to resist the occupation—as on the West Bank, where middle-class Palestinians began to identify with young demon-

In November of that same year, Arafat, wearing a *Keffiyeh* headdress, spoke before the UN General Assembly about his dreams for a Palestinian state. Arafat indicated that the Palestinians wished to establish national authority in both the West Bank and the Gaza Strip, at that time occupied by Israel. He acknowledged Israel's right to exist but referred to the need for "a little homeland of our own." Arafat warned, "I have come bearing an olive branch and a freedom fighter's gun. Do not let the olive branch fall from my hand."*

Forced out of Beirut, where Arafat and the PLO resided until the organization's expulsion in 1982, the Chairman, as he was known, acquired greater stature in late 1988 when he offered a Palestinian peace initiative before the UN General Assembly in Geneva. Declaring his acceptance of Resolution 242, Arafat promised, "The PLO will seek a comprehensive settlement among the parties concerned in the Arab-Israeli conflict, including the State of Palestine, Israel and other neighbors."** In mid-November 1988, the Palestine National Council (PNC) urged the formation of "a provisional government for the State of Palestine." The following March, Arafat was named "president of the state."***

---

*Quoted in Blaine T. Browne and Robert C. Cottrell, *Uncertain Order: The World in the Twentieth Century*. Upper Saddle River, NJ: Prentice Hall, 2002, p. 411.

**Ibid., p. 413.

***Ibid., p. 414.

strators who were residing in refugee camps. Palestinians boycotted Israeli goods and refused to pay the taxes that covered the cost of occupation. Violence escalated all around, with Palestinians wielding knives and grenades more freely; the Israelis in turn employed riot sticks, rubber and plastic bullets, and snipers; confiscated homes; and deported hundreds from both Gaza and the West Bank. Israel also attacked PLO officials outside Israel, from Cyrus to Tunis. By the close of 1989, the Intifada and the reaction to it had resulted in 626 Palestinian and 43 Israeli deaths, tens of thousands of injuries to Arabs, and as many as 40,000 arrests. As hopes for a diplomatic resolution diminished, the PLO, particularly Al-Fatah, increasingly lost influence; Hamas resorted more and more frequently to the assassination of Israelis and the murder of Palestinians viewed as collaborators. The Intifada largely ceased operations in 1991, although acts of violence, many conducted by Islamic fundamentalists, continued in the occupied territories held by Israel.

Even so, the Intifada helped revitalize the PLO, which declared its readiness to negotiate with Israel provided that mutual recognition was forthcoming. Islamic organizations condemned the PLO for its apparent willingness to accept less than the entirety of Palestine. Jordan's King Hussein renounced his claim to the West Bank, enabling the PLO to strengthen its claim to leadership there. The Intifada produced major changes in the territories and Israel, where public debate became more polarized, and catapulted the Palestinian dilemma to the forefront of international politics.

The Intifada itself proved inconclusive, with the Israelis still in control of the territories and the Palestinians demanding self-rule. The PLO did move to recognize Israel and set up a self-governing authority in a relatively small sector of Palestine; Israel recognized the PLO and promised to evacuate from the West Bank and Gaza and return closer to the Green Line. Israeli leftists increasingly insisted that Israel had to abandon the territories beyond the Green Line and accept a two-state solution, although many on the right bitterly condemned leading opponents and favored the transfer of Arab populations. Israel had been fortunate, Benny Morris points out, that Israeli Arab leaders had dissuaded their communities from supporting the Intifada more directly. Thus, they officially condemned violence, ensuring that the Intifada did not move across the Green Line. By contrast, Iraqi Scud missiles tore into Israel during the Gulf War in 1991 but resulted in little damage. Both the PLO and Jordan had backed the losing side—Saddam Hussein's Iraq—during that conflict, which led to still closer relations between Israel, with its seemingly ever-shifting arbitrary borders, and the United States.

10

Oslo and
Porous Borders

At the conclusion of the Gulf War, U.S. President George H. W. Bush and Secretary of State James Baker sought to help resolve the conflicts involving Israel, Arab states, and the Palestinians. Israeli Prime Minister Shamir, Hamas, the PFLP, and the Islamic Jihad all opposed the peace process, which was initiated at an international conference in Madrid co-chaired by Bush and Mikhail Gorbachev, president of the crumbling Soviet Union. The talks in Madrid relied on UN Resolutions 242 and 338, along with the Camp David Accords, to open negotiations. In June 1992, general election results in Israel produced a resounding defeat for Shamir's Likud party, with the Labor party and Yitzhak Rabin able to form a coalition government, along with the left-wing *Meretz* party and the ultra-Orthodox *Shas* party.

Rabin proclaimed his commitment to swapping land beyond the Green Line for peace, which Shamir had rejected. Unofficial discussions with the PLO occurred, some initiated by Yossi Beilin, a Labor representative in the Knesset and a protégé of Foreign Minister Shimon Peres. Although allowing for those meetings, Rabin moved against Palestinian terrorists and Hizbollah in Lebanon, declaring that he would "fight terrorism as if there was no peace process and pursue the peace process as if there was no terrorism."[71] In March 1993, Israel acted to seal the border with Gaza, which threw vast numbers of Palestinians out of work, and suggested drawing back to the Green Line. In July, the IDF conducted extensive assaults against Hizbollah strongholds in southern Lebanon, driving nearly 300,000 villagers northward.

The months ahead witnessed the hammering out of an Israeli-Palestinian accord, the Declaration of Principles, agreed to in Oslo, Norway, on August 20, and Letters of Mutual Recognition. The PLO acknowledged "the right of the State of Israel to exist in peace and security," in addition to UN resolutions 242 and 338.[72] On September 9, Arafat affirmed the PLO's renunciation of terrorism, while indicating that the PLO no longer desired to overthrow Israel through armed struggle.

Rabin responded, stating that his government would acknowl-
edge the PLO as the representative of the Palestinians and would
undertake negotiations with that organization. Israel did not,
however, recognize the right of the Palestinians to a state. Still, a
Palestinian interim self-governing authority (PA), made up of an
elected council, was to be created for both Gaza and the West
Bank and would represent them for the next five years. Israel
promised to dissolve its civil administration and to withdraw its
military government, but the Jewish state retained responsibility
for external security beyond the Green Line as well as for internal security pertaining to the settlements and Israeli citizens.

YITZHAK RABIN

Yitzhak Rabin was born in Jerusalem on March 1, 1922, the son of Nehemiah
Rabin, an American immigrant who had served with the Jewish legion during
World War I, and Rosa, who was one of the initial members of the Haganah.
After graduation from the Kadoorie Agricultural School, Yitzhak Rabin also
joined the Haganah after being inducted by Moshe Dayan. Rabin volunteered
for the Palmah, the Jewish commando force, quickly receiving a promotion to
platoon leader; in 1945, Rabin helped lead an operation that liberated 200 illegal immigrants held in the Atlit detention camp. On "Black Saturday," June 29,
1946, British paratroopers arrested Rabin, along with many other Jewish
leaders, subsequently transporting them temporarily to a British detention
camp in Rafah. Named the Palmah's deputy commander in October 1947,
Rabin helped liberate portions of Jerusalem during the 1948–1949 Arab-
Israeli War and headed military operations on the Southern front that resulted
in Israeli control of the Negev and Eliat. In early 1949, Rabin traveled to
Rhodes, where he represented the Southern front at the armistice talks with
Egypt, which led to the setting of arbitrary borders for the Jewish state.

Shortly after graduating from Great Britain's Staff College in 1953, Rabin
was named brigadier general and received additional high-level appoint-
ments before becoming IDF chief of staff on January 1, 1964. Acting in that
capacity, Rabin, notwithstanding a temporary absence caused by something
of a breakdown, helped guide Israel to the stunning victory in the Six-Day

Terrorism intensified once again in 1994. On February 24, 1994, Baruch Golstein, a settler doctor who supported the right-wing extremist Meir Kahane, murdered at least 29 Muslims who were worshipping in a mosque in Hebron located in a cave also revered by Jews, the Tomb of the Patriarchs. Suicide bombers struck in Israeli cities and towns, with a member of Hamas detonating himself on a bus in downtown Tel Aviv, killing 21. A pair from Islamic Jihad, wearing IDF uniforms, blew up a refreshment stand outside Netanya, killing 22 soldiers. Right-wing demonstrators condemned the prime minister, deeming Rabin a traitor. Again drawing on biblical accounts supposedly attesting

War; that triumph, of course, enabled the Jewish state to expand well beyond the Green Line, which had unforeseen consequences. After leaving the military in early 1968, Rabin became Israel's ambassador to the United States. After his return to Israel in 1973, Rabin entered the Knesset as a Labor party member and was soon named minister of labor. When Prime Minister Golda Meir resigned on June 2, 1974, in the aftermath of the October War, Rabin replaced her, proceeding to shape disengagement accords with both Egypt and Syria. Political difficulties induced Rabin to resign in April 1977, but he was soon back in the Knesset representing the Labor party. During the period of the national unity governments of Shamir and Peres (1984–1990), Rabin, acting as Israel's minister of defense, called for the pullback of Israeli Defense Forces from Lebanon and the fixing of a security zone.

In July 1992, Rabin once again formed a government, simultaneously holding the titles of prime minister and defense minister. During his second term as prime minister, Rabin helped shape the Oslo Accords, signed a peace treaty with Jordan, and moved to turn over control of portions of the West Bank to the Palestine Authority. His efforts on behalf of achieving peace in the Middle East, which seemed to suggest the need for Israel's eventual withdrawal to the Green Line, led to Rabin's receipt of the 1994 Nobel Prize for Peace (shared with Peres and Arafat). On November 4, 1995, after participating in a massive peace rally and in the midst of a barrage of vicious tirades directed at him, Rabin was murdered by a right-wing settler, stunning his followers and leaving the then-governing Labor party bereft.

to the breadth of their land, they insisted that Israel hold on to the West Bank, Judea, and Samaria, all situated beyond the Green Line. The transference of territory enabled Hamas and Islamic Jihad to use the Gaza Strip and Jericho as staging points, to the dismay of many Israelis, who blamed Prime Minister Rabin and Foreign Minister Peres. Many also condemned Arafat, insisting that he prevent terrorist strikes. The IDF moved to close off the border with Gaza, resulting in a severe loss of jobs for Palestinians. Rabin urged that separation from the Palestinians occur and declared that Israel would keep control of Jerusalem and territory near the Jordan River.

In spite of all the difficulties, movement toward providing more secure borders for Israel continued. On October 26, 1994, Israel and Jordan signed a "Treaty of Peace" in the Arava, with an acknowledgement of each nation's right "to live in peace ... within secure and recognized boundaries."[73] Israel relinquished control over approximately 300 square kilometers of land in the Arava and allowed Jordan to draw from the region's northern water resources, as Jordan allowed Israel to acquire water in the Arava. During meetings in March 1995, the Syrians agreed to pull back their military forces further from a future arbitrary border than would the Israelis; Israel offered the possibility of returning to the 1949 border, or Green Line. Syria wanted a withdrawal to the borders that existed prior to the Six-Day War, which would have compelled Israel to cede small amounts of territory, including a northeastern shoreline along the Sea of Galilee. Pressured by Syria, Lebanon proved unable to negotiate withdrawal of IDF units from the security zone.

Talks also continued between the Israelis and the PLO, leading to another agreement, the "Israeli-Palestinian Interim Agreement on the West Bank and Gaza Strip," or Oslo II, which was signed in Washington, D.C., on September 28, 1995, by Rabin, Peres, and Arafat. Under Oslo II, elections were to take place in the territories, with the staggered redeployment of IDF units out of the West Bank. Israeli troops would continue to safeguard Jewish sectors of Hebron, Jewish settlements, military installations, and border areas along the old Green Line in Gaza and the West Bank. Three areas of control were established for the West Bank: (1) Area A or evacuated cities, to be provided security by the Palestinian Authority; (2) Area B, involving most Arab towns and villages, to experience civil authority by the PA but overall security by Israel; and (3) Area C, the less populated West Bank lands, Jewish settlements, and military sites, to be afforded security by Israel, with the PA to offer medical and educational services for Arabs. The PA police began to replace IDF units in major West Bank communities, including Jenin, Nablus, Ramallah-El Bireh, and Bethlehem.

Religious leaders and top figures of the Israeli political right, such as Benjamin Netanyahu and Ariel Sharon, blasted the Oslo Agreements and the prime minister, referring to Rabin in highly denigrating ways. Peace advocates, including members of the Labor party, *Meretz*, and Peace Now, responded by holding a massive demonstration on November 4, 1995, in Kings of Israel Square in downtown Tel Aviv. At the close of the rally, with some 100,000 in attendance, Yigal Amir, a young law student at a religious university and a strong advocate of Jewish settlements beyond the Green Line, assassinated Rabin.

The next national election in Israel occurred in the midst of a wave of terrorist bombings by Hamas and Islamic Jihad and shellings by Hizbollah along the Lebanese border and against Jewish settlements. The Likud party was the political beneficiary of the resulting uncertainty, leading to the formation of a government by Prime Minister Netanyahu. Israeli troop withdrawals and negotiations now lagged, although Netanyahu and Arafat signed an accord on January 14, 1997, that called for Israel to withdraw from most of Hebron, joint Palestinian-Israeli patrols around Hebron, and the safeguarding of Jewish areas. The Hebron Agreement also allowed for the release of various prisoners, the opening of airports and seaports in Gaza, the redeployment of additional IDF units from the West Bank, and the quashing of a terrorist infrastructure in territories controlled by the PA.

Little further progress ensued during 1997, as a series of crippling suicide attacks by Hamas occurred in Jerusalem and the Netanyahu government did not withdraw IDF units from additional rural areas in the West Bank. Notwithstanding pressure by U.S. President Bill Clinton, Israel failed to adhere to various promises, including the release of additional prisoners and the opening up of airports and seaports in Gaza. Moreover, the PA did nothing to rein in Hamas or bring terrorism to a halt. By February 1998, Netanyahu did agree to withdraw the IDF from 13 percent of the West Bank, but only in a staged fashion that had to be preceded by Palestinian concessions. Meeting at the White House on October 23, 1998, Netanyahu and Arafat, with Clinton and King Hussein in attendance, signed an agreement, the Wye River Memorandum, which indicated that Israel would relinquish various amounts of territory on the West Bank. Both sides agreed to work to halt terrorism, with the Palestinians promising to arrest terrorist suspects. Pressured by right-wing members of his own coalition, Netanyahu subsequently suspended the IDF withdrawals.

At the same time, Netanyahu, relying on a Jewish-American friend as a go-between, considered the possibility of moving the IDF back to either the 1923 international border or a point based on conditions prior to the Six-Day War. Syrian President Assad, in turn, accepted the idea of establishing early warning stations operated by Americans or Frenchmen, in addition to Israelis, and of pulling his troops farther away from Israel. Opposition by members of Likud, spearheaded by Ariel Sharon, forced a halt to these discussions.

In May 1999, Labor's Ehud Barak easily defeated Netanyahu in the Israeli general elections, leading to hopes for improved relations with both Palestinians and Arab states. Barak promised Arafat that Israel would abide by the Wye memorandum, while calling for a full peace accord. On September 4, 1999, Barak and Arafat signed the Sharm al-Sheikh Agreement, which called for additional Israeli withdrawals from the West Bank, the release of 350 Palestinian prisoners, and the initiation of negotiations producing a final peace settlement predicated on UN resolutions 242 and 338. After the prisoners were released and Israel began its withdrawal, the two sides wrestled over the amount of territory that was to be ceded to the Palestinians. Not helping matters was the outbreak of a series of terrorist strikes by Palestinians inside Israel. The continued construction of Jewish settlements beyond the Green Line convinced the Palestinians to halt negotiations.

Although the negotiations with the PLO stalled, Barak continued another series of talks involving Israel's northern borders. With encouragement from President Clinton, the Israelis and Syrians drafted a peace treaty that eventually pushed most Israeli forces back to the pre-1967 borders. Talks ended with the Syrians insisting on a return to the northeastern waterline of the Sea of Galilee and emboldened Hizbollah attacks in Lebanon's security zone. Despite opposition from IDF commanders, the Israeli government, fulfilling a campaign promise of Barak's, voted to withdraw from South Lebanon, moving back to the international border by July 2000. The IDF built up a mined fence, complete with electronic sensors, along the frontier established by British and French administrators in 1923, as mandated by UN Resolution 425. At the frontier's northeastern sector, Israel did retain control of approximately 20 square kilometers of land that had been taken after the Six-Day War and during the battle against the PLO. With the collapse of the Southern Lebanese Army, Hizbollah moved to control the security zone.

Another round of negotiations involving the West Bank occurred during the final months of Clinton's presidency. In March 2000, Barak agreed to deliver hundreds of square kilometers of territory encircling Jericho, Ramallah, and Jenin but refused to relinquish Anabta and Abu Dis, which arguably composed part of East Jerusalem. As new talks began at Camp David in July, a host of issues continued to divide the parties: the question of refugees and the so-called right of return, dating back to the dispossession that occurred during the 1948–1949 war; control over the West Bank and Gaza; the fate of Jerusalem and the settlements; water rights; and future borders.

Barak appeared willing to cede 90 percent of the West Bank and virtually all of Gaza, but the talks broke down. Instead, a second Intifada began, termed the *al-Aqsa Intifada* by Palestinians. On September 28, Ariel Sharon, the Likud party's new chairman, along with scores of policemen, visited the Temple Mount. Angry Muslims rioted, stoning Israeli police stationed close to the religious site. Another riot broke out the next day, resulting in the shooting by police of at least four Palestinians and the wounding of many more. Throughout many sectors of Jerusalem, rioting occurred, following clashes on the West Bank and in Gaza, pitting demonstrators against Israeli soldiers. The PA incited matters further by warning of an attack against Jerusalem and urging a jihad. This time, rioters employed not merely stones but light weapons and bombs and were soon joined by Israeli Arabs. Increasingly, the PA appeared either helpless or complicit regarding the violence that was unfolding. Other groups, including Hamas and Islamic Jihad, acquired larger followings on the West Bank and Gaza. Israel began targeting leaders of these groups for assassination, in addition to razing fields and houses.

Ironically, the first several months of the second Intifada led to another round of peace talks, with the Clinton-orchestrated proposals calling for delivery of approximately 95 percent of the West Bank to the Palestinians. Israel would further compensate Palestinians by relinquishing additional territory. The new borders, close to the original Green Line, would be manned by an international peacekeeping force. Although Barak reluctantly accepted the plan, Arafat rejected it. Additional efforts at peacekeeping similarly failed, helping ensure Barak's resounding defeat in the February 2001 general elections.

The victor of the 2001 election was Ariel Sharon, the hardline leader of the Likud party, who relied on an iron-fist policy to end violence in the territories and throughout Israel, which soon suffered the worst spate of terrorism yet. Rejecting both Oslo II and Barak's proposals, Sharon eventually discussed relinquishing just over 40 percent of the occupied territory beyond

Decades after the creation of Israel, terrorism and violence continue between Israelis and Palestinians. Here, an Israeli soldier supervises the construction of a concrete wall separating Israel from the Palestinian West Bank. Israel hoped the wall would keep the country safe from Palestinian terrorist bombings.

the Green Line but none of Jerusalem. Seeking to put pressure on Arafat, Sharon sent IDF units to batter the PLA leader's compound in Ramallah, while pounding areas on the West Bank and in Gaza considered receptive to violence being directed against Israelis. Then, in June 2002, after a series of suicide bombings, Israel began constructing a separation barrier intended to cover 225 miles and to run largely along the Green Line, on the West Bank. Right-wing Israelis worried that the building of the wall would ensure the establishment of a Palestinian state and the displacement of 200,000 Jewish settlers. Palestinians condemned the barrier, warning that it cut through towns, villages, and farmland, while further dividing the West Bank.

As violence continued to mount, three campaigns sought to bring resolution to the Palestinian situation and to ensure a restoration of the Green Line. Increasingly concerned about terrorism in the wake of the September 11, 2001, attacks on the World Trade Center and the Pentagon, the United States joined with the United Nations, Russia, and the European Union in supporting a road map to peace in the Middle East. This proposal was intended to produce an independent Palestinian state with its own borders by the end of 2005 but was rejected by Sharon.

The Israeli prime minister was no happier with two other proposals: the People's Voice and the Geneva Accord. The Peoples' Voice, sponsored by Ami Ayalon, who had headed the *Shin Bet* (the Israeli General Security Service), and Sari Nusseibeh, the Arab head of Al-Quds University, urged a two-state solution, which required a general Israeli withdrawal from the territories beyond the Green Line and creation of a Palestinian state. Spurred by former Israeli Justice Minister Yossi Beilin and former Palestinian Information Minister Yasser Abed Rabbo, talks between Israelis and Palestinians led to calls for a Geneva Accord that would draw on the Camp David and Oslo resolutions. This proposal affirmed belief in "a two-state solution based on UNSC Resolutions 242 and 338," the right of both the Jewish people and the Palestinian people to statehood within distinct arbitrary boundaries, and "the right to peaceful and secure existence within secure and recognized boundaries free from threats or acts of force." The arbitrary border between the Jewish and Palestinian states, the Geneva Accord declared, would "be based on the June 4th 1967 lines with reciprocal modifications on a 1:1 basis." Both sides agreed "to reject and condemn terrorism and violence in all its forms," to respect human rights, and to allow security guarantees to be provided by a multinational force.[74] Jerusalem would be the capital of the two states, with a multinational force to guard the Temple Mount; the Wailing Wall would remain under Israeli sovereignty, free movement would be allowed in the Old City, and the Israelis would administer the Mount of Olives Ceremony and the Western Wall Tunnel.

Israeli Prime Minister Sharon condemned the Geneva Accord as "the most historic, tragic mistake since the failed Oslo Accords."[75] In early January 2004, Palestinian Prime Minister

Ahmed Qureia warned that Palestinians would opt for a binational approach if Israel retained control of sections of the West Bank. Qureia criticized the building of the separation barrier: "This is an apartheid solution to put the Palestinians in cantons. Who can accept this?" The wall, Qureia warned, "is to unilaterally mark the borders, this is the intention behind the wall ... It will kill the road map and kill the two-state vision."[76] The United States, Secretary of State Colin Powell reported, remained committed to the two-state solution, leading Sharon to deliver a speech in Herzliyah indicating a readiness to remove various settlements to help implement the road map.

Another leading member of the Likud party, Deputy Prime Minister and Minister of Trade and Industry Ehud Olmert, urged a unilateral withdrawal from most of the West Bank and Gaza and a pullback to the Green Line. Like a growing number of his fellow Israelis, Olmert worried that the Arab population would soon outnumber the Jewish one in Israel and the occupied territories. Olmert declared, "When we faced the choice of a complete land without a Jewish state, or a Jewish state without the complete land, we chose a Jewish state."[77]

For more than half a century following establishment of the nation of Israel, its very makeup remained in question. From the time of the initial United Nations' mandate calling for the creation of a Jewish nation, there had been many in the Arab world adverse to that very possibility; that antagonism, in fact, had lengthier roots, reaching back additional generations. After the Jewish state was established, hostilities continued to break out, frequently resulting in an expansion of Israel's boundaries, to the dismay of its Arab neighbors and many non-Jewish Palestinians. Israel thus experienced the constant alteration of the arbitrary borders that defined it geographically.

Those borders shifted most dramatically after the 1948-1949 Arab-Israeli War, which produced the Green Line, and then again following the Six-Day War, when Israel occupied territories well beyond that artificial frontier. Those two conflicts in particular led to large numbers of refugees, charges of dispossession, and, inevitably, terrorist activities. Too often forgotten was that in addition to Palestinian refugees, almost 856,000 *Mizrahi* Jews, from throughout North African and Middle Eastern Arab countries, existed. Those Jews suffered the loss of property, employment, and basic human rights, when they were compelled to depart from Algeria, Egypt, Iraq, Lebanon, Morocco, Syria, Tunisia, and Yemen, over a span of three decades, starting with the 1948–1949 Arab-Israeli War. In 2003, U.S. House Resolution 311 urged acknowledgment of the Mizrahi Jews who "fled Arab countries because they faced a campaign of ethnic cleansing and were forced to leave behind land, private homes, personal effects, businesses, community assets and thousands of years of their Jewish heritage and history."[78]

All of this resulted in a conundrum for the Middle East's lone democratic state, remarkably stable in many ways, but continually grappling with arbitrary borders that were affected by historical developments, religious fervor, and nationalistic hopes and expectations. At the same time, there remained the simple fact that peoples with disparate hopes, dreams, and visions aspired to control the same small patch of land, revered by Jews, Muslims, and Christians. Repeatedly, the Green Line ringing that territory stood as both a starting point for discussion and a matter of great contention, as arbitrary borders frequently do.

c. 3000 B.C.	The Canaanites settle ancient Palestine.
c. 1250 B.C.	The Jews conquer Canaan.
c. 1000 B.C.	The Jews defeat the Philistines and the Canaanites and establish the Kingdom of Israel.
c. 950 B.C.	King Solomon builds the first temple in Jerusalem.
928 B.C.	The Kingdom of Israel is divided into the kingdoms of Israel in the north and Judea in the south.
721 B.C.	The Assyrians conquer the kingdom of Israel.
586 B.C.	The Babylonians under Nebuchadnezzar defeat Judah, deport dignitaries, and destroy the First Temple.
539 B.C.	The Persians defeat the Babylonians and allow Jews to return to southern Palestine and to rebuild the Temple.
333 B.C.	Alexander the Great defeats Persia, resulting in the Greek takeover of Palestine.
323 B.C.	After the death of Alexander the Great, Palestine is ruled by the Egyptian Ptolemies and the Syrian Seleucids.
165 B.C.	The Maccabees revolt against Antiochus Epiphanes, establishing an independent state (under the Hasmonean Dynasty).
63 B.C.	The Romans conquer Palestine.
A.D. 66–73	Jewish revolt occurs, concluding with the mass suicide at Massada in A.D. 73. The Romans level Jerusalem and destroy the Second Temple.
132–135	Bar Kokhba leads a mass uprising against Roman rule, but resulting retaliation leads to exile and the diaspora.
330	Byzantinian rule of Palestine begins.
638	Muslims take control of Palestine. Omar ibn al-Khattaab leads Muslim forces into Jerusalem. With various exceptions, Muslims rule Palestine until 1918.
661	Umayyad chaliphs from Damascus govern Palestine and soon undertake the construction of the Dome of the Rock.
750	The Abbasid caliphs govern Palestine.
969	The Fatimids (from Egypt) govern Palestine.

1071	The Saljuqs (from Isfahan) govern Jerusalem and various sections of Palestine.
1099	The Crusaders set up the Latin Kingdom of Jerusalem.
1187	Kurdistan's Salah al-Diin al-Ayyoubi defeats the crusaders at the battle of Hittin. Henceforth, Cairo governs Palestine.
1260	The Mamluks replace the Ayybis as the rulers of Palestine.
1516	The Ottoman Empire takes control of Palestine.
1832	The Egyptian Moh'd Ali Pasha governs Palestine.
1840	The Ottomans reestablish control over Palestine.
1878	Zionists establish their first settlement, Petach Tiqva.
1882	The first mass illegal Zionist immigration begins.
1896	Theodore Herzl publishes *Der Judenstaat* (*The Jewish State*).

c. 1000 B.C.
Jews defeat the Philistines and the Canaanites, and establish the Kingdom of Israel

1882
The first mass illegal Zionist immigration begins

1939
World War II and the Holocaust begin

132–135
Bar Kokhba leads uprising against Roman rule, but retaliation leads to exile and the diaspora

1917
The Balfour Declaration is issued

c. 1000 B.C.

1947

638
Muslims take control of Palestine and rule Palestine until 1918

66–73 A.D.
Jewish revolt occurs, concluding with the mass suicide at Massada in 73 A.D.

1896
Theodore Herzl publishes *Der Judenstaat* (*The Jewish State*)

1947
The UN General Assembly approves of partitioning Palestine and war breaks out

1897	The World Zionist Organization presents the Basle Program, urging the establishment of a Jewish homeland in Palestine, and the World Zionist Organization.
1901	The Jewish National Fund is established.
1904	The second mass illegal Zionist immigration starts.
1909	Zionists set up the first Zionist kibbutz and begin establishing Tel Aviv.
1916	The Sykes-Picot Agreement is issued. The Arab revolt begins.
1917	The Balfour Declaration is issued.
1918	British General Allenby takes control of Jerusalem. The Faysal-Weizmann Agreement is issued.
1919	The third mass Zionist immigration begins.
1920	The Histadrut is established. Disturbances break out in Palestine.

1948
David Ben-Gurion proclaims the State of Israel and the 1948–1949 Arab-Israeli War Begins

1993
The Israeli-Palestinian Declaration of Principles is signed in Oslo and Washington, D.C.

1956
Israel, Britain, and France invade Egypt

1973
The October or *Yom Kippur* War takes place. The UN issues Resolution 338

2000
The Second *Intifada* begins

1948   **2000**

1949
Armistice talks bring about truces between Israel and Egypt, Lebanon, Jordan, and Syria. The Green Line is established

1967
The Six-Day War unfolds, resulting in Israeli occupation of the Sinai, Gaza, the West Bank, East Jerusalem, and the Golan Heights. The UN issues Resolution 242

1978
Israel invades south Lebanon. The Camp David Accords are issued

1987
The First *Intifada* begins

115

1921	Zionists establish the Haganah. Haji Amin al-Husayni becomes the Mufti of Jerusalem.
1922	The League of Nations approves the British mandate over Palestine.
1923	The British mandate officially begins.
1924	The fourth wave of Zionist immigration starts.
1925	Vladimir Jabotinsky urges the establishment of a Jewish state in Palestine.
1929	Zionist claims to the Western Wall result in riots by Muslims. The fifth wave of immigration begins.
1931	The Irgun, led by Jabotinsky, is formed.
1933	Adolph Hitler's takeover of Germany begins.
1935	Zionist revisionists depart from the World Zoroastrian Organization, calling for the liberation of Palestine and East Jordan.
1936	The Arab Revolt begins.
1937	The Peel Commission calls for the partitioning of Palestine. The Arab Higher Committee rejects the Peel Commission report.
1939	British White Paper calls for the establishment of a Palestinian state after 10 years and restricts Jewish immigration. World War II and the Holocaust begin. Separatists secede from the Irgun and form the Stern Gang.
1940	The sixth wave of Zionist immigration occurs.
1942	The Baltimore Conference urges "making Palestine a Jewish homeland."
1944	Arab leaders issue the Alexandria Protocol. The Haganah moves against the Irgun and Lehi.
1946	U.S. President Truman calls for Palestine to admit 100,000 Jewish refugees. The Irgun blows up the King David Hotel in Jerusalem.
1947	The Arab League denounces partitioning, which the Jewish Agency accepts. The UN General Assembly approves of partitioning Palestine. War breaks out, pitting Jews against Palestinians and Arab states.
1948	The Irgun and Lehi carry out a massacre in Dayr Yasin, and Arabs retaliate against a Jewish medical convoy. David Ben-Gurion proclaims the

establishment of the State of Israel. The 1948–1949 Arab-Israeli War begins. Lehi assassins murder UN mediator Count Folke Bernadotte. King Abdullah proclaims the establishment of the kingdom of Jordan, uniting Trans-Jordan and Arab Palestine.

1949	Armistice talks bring about truces between Israel and the Arab states it warred with: Egypt, Lebanon, Jordan, and Syria.
1950	Israel proclaims the Law of Return. Jordan unites the East Bank and the remainder of the West Bank.
1951	A Palestinian murders King Abdullah.
1954	Gamal Abdul Nasser takes power in Egypt.
1956	Nasser nationalizes the Suez Canal. Israel, Great Britain, and France invade Egypt.
1957	Israel withdraws from the Sinai and Gaza.
1959	Al-Fatah is founded.
1964	The Palestine Liberation Organization (PLO) is founded.
1965	Al-Fatah conducts raids against Israel.
1967	The Six-Day War unfolds, resulting in Israeli occupation of the Sinai, Gaza, the West Bank, East Jerusalem, and the Golan Heights. The UN issues Resolution 242.
1968	The Labor party is founded. The Popular Front for the Liberation of Palestine (PFLP) is founded.
1969	Egypt and Israel begin a war of attrition. Yasir Arafat becomes PLO chairman.
1970	Jordan experiences civil war.
1971	The PLO is forced to relocate to Lebanon.
1972	Black September murders Israeli athletes and coaches at the Munich Olympics.
1973	The Likud party is founded. The October, or Yom Kippur, War takes place. The UN issues Resolution 338.
1974	The Arab League accepts the PLO as "the sole legitimate representative of the Palestinian people." Arafat addresses the UN General Assembly.
1977	Menachem Begin becomes prime minister of Israel.

1978	Israeli invades south Lebanon. The Camp David Accords are issued.
1979	The Egyptian-Israeli Peace Treaty is issued.
1981	Israel annexes the Golan Heights. An Egyptian fundamentalist assassinates Sadat.
1982	Israel invades Lebanon. The Sabra and Shatila massacres occur.
1984	Israeli coalition governments begin.
1987	The first Intifada begins.
1988	Jordan disengages from the West Bank. Hamas is founded.
1991	The Gulf War takes place. Arab-Israeli discussions occur in Madrid. The Soviet Union dissolves.
1992	Labor wins the Israeli general elections; Yitzhak Rabin becomes prime minister.
1993	The United States brokers a cease-fire between Israel and Hizbollah. The Israeli-Palestinian Declaration of Principles is signed in Oslo and Washington, D.C.
1994	Palestinian self-rule starts in Gaza and Jericho. The Jordan-Israel Peace Treaty is signed.
1995	Oslo II is signed in Washington, D.C. A right-wing Israeli settler assassinates Rabin.
1996	The Palestinian self-governing authority is elected.
1997	The Hebron Redeployment Agreement is signed.
1998	The Wye Memorandum is signed.
1999	The Sharm al-Sheikh Agreement is signed.
2000	The second Intifada begins.
2001	Ariel Sharon is elected prime minister of Israel.
2002	Israel begins construction of a separation barrier.
2003	Proposals are issued in the form of the People's Voice and the "Geneva Accord."
2004	Palestinians threaten to support a bi-national solution.

Chapter 1

1. Quoted in Benny Morris, *Righteous Victims: A History of the Zionist-Arab Conflict, 1881–2001.* New York: Vintage Books, 2001, p. 251.
2. Ibid., p. 252.
3. Quoted in *Moshe Dayan, Moshe Dayan: Story of My Life.* New York: William Morrow and Company, Inc., 1976, p. 133.
4. Quoted in Tom Segev, *1949: The First Israelis.* New York: Owl Books, 1998, p. 8.
5. Quoted in Dayan, p. 135.
6. Ibid., p. 136.
7. Ibid., p. 138.
8. Ibid., p. 139.
9. Quoted in "Paving the Way to Peace in Palestine: Significance of Israel–Trans-Jordan Armistice," *United Nations Bulletin* 6, April 15, 1949, p. 385.
10. Ibid.
11. Ibid.
12. Quoted in "Jordanian-Israeli General Armistice Agreement, April 3, 1949," *Middle East Historical Documents,* http://www.mideastweb.org/isrjo-rarmistice1949.htm. Online.
13. Ibid.
14. Ibid.
15. Quoted in "Paving the Way to Peace in Palestine," p. 385.
16. Quoted in Segev,. p. 21.

Chapter 2

17. Quoted in Charles D. Smith, *Palestine and the Arab-Israeli Conflict.* New York: St. Martin's Press, 2001, p. 2.
18. Quoted in J. M. Roberts, *A Short History of the World.* New York: Oxford University Press, 1997, p. 162.
19. Quoted in Eli Barnavi, ed., *A Historical Atlas of the Jewish People: From the Time of the Patriarchs to the Present.* New York: Schocken Books, 1992, p. 108.

Chapter 3

20. Quoted in Theodore Herzl, *The Jewish State.* New York: Dover Publications, 1989.
21. Quoted in Joseph Telushkin, *Jewish Literacy: The Most Important Things to Know About the Jewish Religion, Its People,*

and Its History. New York: William Morrow and Company, Inc., 1991, p. 267.
22. Quoted in Barnavi, p. 221.
23. Quoted in Smith, p. 43.
24. Quoted in Yosef Gorny, *Zionism and the Arabs 1882–1948: A Study of Ideology.* Oxford: Clarendon Press, 1987, p. 22.
25. Quoted in "The Balfour Declaration November 2, 1917," *Middle East Historical Documents,* http://www.mideastweb.org/isrjo-rarmistice1949.htm. Online.
26. Ibid.
27. Quoted in Smith, p. 83.
28. Ibid., p. 84.
29. Quoted in "The Churchill White Paper," in Smith, p. 156.
30. Quoted in Smith, p. 119.
31. Ibid., p. 131.
32. Quoted in "The Peel Commission Partition Plans 1938," *Middle East Historical Documents,* http://www.mideastweb.org/isrjo-rarmistice1949.htm. Online.
33. Ibid.
34. Quoted in Morris, p. 158.

Chapter 4

35. Quoted in Dan Kurzman, *Ben-Gurion: Prophet of Fire.* New York: Simon and Schuster, 1983, p. 227.
36. Quoted in Morris, p. 168.
37. Quoted in "What Happened at the Zionist Biltmore Conference in May 1942?" http://www.palestinefacts.org/pf_man-date_biltmore.php. Online.
38. Quoted in Ritchie Ovendale, *Britain, the United States, and the End of the Palestine Mandate, 1942–1948.* Suffolk: The Royal Historical Society, 1989, p. 33.
39. Quoted in Kurzman, p. 254.
40. Quoted in "The Alexandria Protocol; October 7, 1944," http://www.yale.edu/lawweb/avalon/mideast/alex.htm. Online.
41. Quoted in Barnavi, p. 242.
42. Quoted in Morris, p. 186.

Chapter 5

43. Quoted in Derek J. Pensler, "To Be a Free Nation...." In Nicholas De Lange, ed., *The Illustrated History of the Jewish People.*

New York: Harcourt Brace & Company, 1997, p. 350.

44. Quoted in Bernard Wasserstein, "The Age of Upheavals." In DeLange, pp. 357–358.

Chapter 6

45. Quoted in "Declaration of the Establishment of the State of Israel May 14, 1948." In Smith, p. 221.
46. Quoted in Telushkin, p. 338.
47. Quoted in Smith, p. 246.
48. Quoted in "The Eisenhower Doctrine on the Middle East, A Message to Congress, January 5, 1957," http://www.fordham.edu/halsall/mod/19 57eisenhowerdoctrine.html. Online.

Chapter 7

49. Quoted in Michael B. Oren, *Six Days of War: June 1967 and the Making of the Modern Middle East.* New York: Oxford University Press, 2002, p. 21.
50. Quoted in Smith, p. 275.
51. Quoted in Oren, p. 28.
52. Ibid.
53. Ibid., p. 45.
54. Ibid., p. 52.
55. Ibid., p. 86.
56. Ibid., p. 89.
57. Quoted in Morris, p. 310.
58. Quoted in Oren, p. 310.

Chapter 8

59. Quoted in Oren, p. 314.
60. Ibid.
61. Quoted in ibid., p. 314.
62. Quoted in Morris, p. 338.
63. Quoted in Smith, p. 304.
64. Quoted in "U. N. Security Council Resolution 242," *Middle East Historical Documents*, http://www.mideastweb.org/242.htm. Online.
65. Quoted in Morris, p. 390.
66. Quoted in Howard Blum, *The Eve of Destruction: The Untold Story of the Yom Kippur War.* New York: HarperCollins Publishers, 2003, p. 190.

Chapter 9

67. Quoted in Morris, p. 440.
68. Quoted in Smith, p. 330.
69. Quoted in "Camp David Accords–1978," *Middle East Historical Documents*, http://www.mideastweb.org/campdavid.h tm. Online.
70. Quoted in Morris, p. 501.

Chapter 10

71. Ibid. p. 617.
72. Quoted in Smith, p. 458.
73. Quoted in "Israel-Jordan Peace Treaty October 26, 1994," *Middle East Historical Documents*, http://www.mideastweb.org/ israjordan.htm. Online.
74. Quoted in "The Geneva Accords," *Middle East Historical Documents*, http://www.mideastweb.org/geneva1.htm. Online.
75. Quoted in Ellis Shuman, "Sharon: 'Geneva Accord' Is Most Historic, Tragic Mistake since Oslo," *Israel Insider*, October 13, 2003.
76. Quoted in Nathan Guttman, "Palestinian PM Says Two-State Solution in Danger," *Haaretz.Com*. Online. January 8, 2004.
77. Quoted in Gershom Gorenberg, "The Cracking of the Israeli Right," *The Jerusalem Report XIV*, December 29, 2003, p. 10.
78 . Jack Epstein, "Jews Who Fled Arab Lands Now Press Their Cause," *San Francisco Chronicle*, March 28, 2004, p. A3.

Books

Angel, Marc D. *The Jews of Rhodes: The History of a Sephardic Community.* New York: Sepher-Hermon Press, Inc. and The Union of Sephardic Congregations, 1978.

Barnavi, Eli, ed. *A Historical Atlas of the Jewish People: From the Time of the Patriarchs to the Present.* New York: Schocken Books, 1992.

Ben-Gurion, David. *Memoirs.* New York: World Publishing, 1970.

Berger, Earl. *The Covenant and the Sword: Arab-Israeli Relations 1948–1956.* London: Routledge & Kegan Paul Ltd, 1965.

Blum, Howard. *The Eve of Destruction: The Untold Story of the Yom Kippur War.* New York: HarperCollins Publishers, 2003.

Bornstein, Avram S. *Crossing the Green Line: Between the West Bank and Israel.* Philadelphia: University of Pennsylvania Press, 2003.

Browne, Blaine T. and Robert C. Cottrell. *Uncertain Order: The World in the Twentieth Century.* Upper Saddle River, NJ: Prentice Hall, 2002.

Dayan, Moshe. Moshe Dayan: *The Story of My Life.* New York: William Morrow and Company, Inc., 1976.

De Lange, Nicholas, ed. *The Illustrated History of the Jewish People.* New York: Harcourt Brace & Company, 1997.

Dicks, Brian. *Rhodes.* Harrisburg, PA: Stackpole Books, 1974.

Fromkin, David. *A Peace to End All Peace: The Fall of the Ottoman Empire and the Creation of the Modern Middle East.* New York: Owl Books, 2001.

Gorney, Yosef. *Zionism and the Arabs 1882–1848: A Study of Ideology.* Oxford: Clarendon Press, 1987.

Herzl, Theodore. *The Jewish State.* New York: Dover Publications, 1989.

Herzog, Chaim. *The Arab-Israeli Wars: War and Peace in the Middle East from the War of Independence through Lebanon.* New York: Vintage Books, 1984.

Kurzman, Dan. *Ben-Gurion: Prophet of Fire.* New York: Simon and Schuster, 1983.

Morris, Benny. *Righteous Victims: A History of the Zionist-Arab Conflict, 1881–2001.* New York: Vintage Books, 2001.

Oren, Michael B. *Six Days of War: June 1967 and the Making of the Modern Middle East.* New York: Oxford University Press, 2002.

Ovendale, Ritchie. *Britain, the United States, and the End of the Palestine Mandate, 1942–1948.* Suffolk: The Royal Historical Society, 1989.

Pappe, Ilan. *A History of Modern Palestine: One Land, Two Peoples.* Cambridge: Cambridge University Press, 2004.

Rabin, Yitzhak. *The Rabin Memoirs.* Boston: Little, Brown and Company, 1979.

Roberts, J. M. *A Short History of the World.* New York: Oxford University Press, 1997.

Segev, Tom. *1949: The First Israelis.* New York: Owl Books, 1998.

_____ *One Palestine, Complete: Jews and Arabs Under the British Mandate.* New York: Owl Books, 2000.

Shlaim, Avi. *The Iron Wall: Israel and the Arab World.* New York: W. W. Norton & Company, 2001.

Smith, Charles D. *Palestine and the Arab-Israeli Conflict.* New York: St. Martin's Press, 2001.

Telushkin, Joseph. *Jewish Literacy: The Most Important Things to Know About the Jewish Religion, Its People, and Its History.* New York: William Morrow, 1991.

Wallach, Janet and John Wallach. *Arafat: In the Eyes of the Beholder.* London: Heinemann, 1990.

Articles and Documents

"The Alexandria Protocol; October 7, 1944," http: //www.yale.edu/lawweb/avalon/mideast/alex.htm. Online.

"The Churchill White Paper." In Smith, Charles D. *Palestine and the Arab-Israeli Conflict.* New York: St. Martin's Press, 2001.

"Declaration of the Establishment of the State of Israel May 14, 1948." In Smith, Charles D. *Palestine and the Arab-Israeli Conflict.* New York: St. Martin's Press, 2001.

"The Eisenhower Doctrine on the Middle East, A Message to Congress, January 5, 1957," http://www.fordham.edu/halsall/mod/1957eisenhowerdoctrine.html. Online.

Epstein, Jack. "Jews Who Fled Arab Lands Now Press Their Cause," *San Francisco Chronicle,* March 28, 2004.

Gorenberg, Gershom. "The Cracking of the Israeli Right." *The Jerusalem Report XIV,* December 29, 2003, p. 10.

Guttman, Nathan. "Palestinian PM Says Two-State Solution in Danger." *Haaretz.com.* Online. January 8, 2004.

"Middle East Historical Documents," http://www.mideastweb.org. Online.

"Paving the Way to Peace in Palestine: Significance of Israel-Trans-Jordan Armistice." *United Nations Bulletin* 6, April 15, 1949, p. 385.

Penslar, Derek J. " 'To Be a Free Nation ...,'" In De Lange, Nicholas, ed. *The Illustrated History of the Jewish People.* New York: Harcourt Brace & Company, 1997, pp. 303–353.

Shuman, Ellis. "Sharon: 'Geneva Accord' Is Most Historic, Tragic Mistake since Oslo," *Israel Insider,* October 13, 2003.

Wasserstein, Bernard. "The Age of Upheavals." In De Lange, Nicholas, ed. *The Illustrated History of the Jewish People.* New York: Harcourt Brace & Company, 1997, pp. 355–397.

"What Happened at the Zionist Biltmore Conference in May 1942?"
http://www.palestinefacts.org/pf_mandate_biltmore.php. Online.

Beilin, Yossi. *Israel: A Concise Political History.* New York: St. Martin's Press, 1993.

Bickerton, Ian J. and Carla L. Klausner. *A Concise History of the Arab-Israeli Conflict,* 3rd ed. Upper Saddle River, NJ: Prentice Hall, 1998.

Efron, Noah J. *Real Jews: Secular vs. Ultra-Orthodox and the Struggle for Jewish Identity in Israel.* New York: Basic Books, 2003.

Farsoun, Samih K. with Christina E. Zacharia. *Palestine and the Palestinians.* Boulder, CO: Westview Press, 1998.

Friedman, Thomas L. *From Beiruit to Jerusalem.* New York: Anchor Books, 1995.

Goldberg, David J. *To the Promised Land: A History of Zionist Thought.* New York: Penguin Books, 1996.

Goldschmidt, A., Jr. *A Concise History of the Middle East,* 4th ed. Boulder, CO: Westview Press, 1991.

Grossman, David. *Death as a Way of Life: Israel Ten Years After Oslo.* New York: Farrar, Straus and Giroux, 2003.

Horovitz, David. *A Little Too Close to God: The Thrills and Panic of a Life in Israel.* New York: Alfred A. Knopf, 2000.

Johnson, Paul. *A History of the Jews.* New York: HarperPerennial, 1988.

Karsh, Efraim. *Arafat's War: The Man and His Battle for Israeli Conquest.* New York: Grove Press, 2003.

Kushner, Tony, and Alisa Solomon, eds. *Wrestling with Zion: Progressive Jewish-American Responses to the Israeli-Palestinian Conflict.* New York: Grove Press, 2003.

La Guardia, Anton. *War Without End: Israelis, Palestinians, and the Struggle for a Promised Land.* New York: Thomas Dunne Books, 2001.

Mandel, Neville J. *The Arabs and Zionism Before World War I.* Berkeley: University of California Press, 1976.

Margalit, Avishai. *Views in Review: Politics and Culture in the State of the Jews.* New York: Farrar, Straus and Giroux, 1998.

Rosenthal, Donna. *The Israelis: Ordinary People in an Extraordinary Land.* New York: Free Press, 2003.

Said, Edward. *Peace and Its Discontents: The Struggle for Palestinian Self-Determination 1969–1994.* London: Vintage, 1995.

Segev, Tom. *The Seventh Million: The Israelis and the Holocaust.* New York: Owl Books, 2000.

Sharon, Ariel, with David Chanoff. *Warrior: An Autobiography.* New York: Simon & Schuster, 2001.

Shipler, David K. *Arab and Jew: Wounded Spirits in a Promised Land.* New York: Penguin Books, 2002.

Tessler, Mark. *A History of the Israeli-Palestinian Conflict.* Bloomington: Indiana University Press, 1994.

page:

Robert C. Cottrell is Professor of History and American Studies at California State University, Chico. He is the author of many books and articles, including *Vietnam: the 17th Parallel, Izzy: A Biography of I.F. Stone, Roger Nash Baldwin and the American Civil Liberties Union, The Best Pitcher in Baseball: the Life of Rube Foster, Negro League Giant,* and *Uncertain Order: The World in the Twentieth Century.* He is the recipient of numerous awards and fellowships, including grants from the National Endowment for the Humanities and the American Philosophical Society. In 1998, he was honored as the Outstanding Professor at CSUC, and in 2000, was named winner of the Wang Family Excellence Award for Social & Behavioral Sciences & Public Services, a systemwide honor for the 23 campuses that make up the California State University.

George J. Mitchell served as chairman of the peace negotiations in Northern Ireland during the 1990s. Under his leadership, an historic accord, ending decades of conflict, was agreed to by the governments of Ireland and the United Kingdom and the political parties in Northern Ireland. In May 1998, the agreement was overwhelmingly endorsed by a referendum of the voters of Ireland, North and South. Senator Mitchell's leadership earned him worldwide praise and a Nobel Peace Prize nomination. He accepted his appointment to the U.S. Senate in 1980. After leaving the Senate, Senator Mitchell joined the Washington, D.C. law firm of Piper Rudnick, where he now practices law. Senator Mitchell's life and career have embodied a deep commitment to public service and he continues to be active in worldwide peace and disarmament efforts.

James I. Matray is professor of history and chair at California State University, Chico. He has published more than forty articles and book chapters on U.S.-Korean relations during and after World War II. Author of *The Reluctant Crusade: American Foreign Policy in Korea, 1941–1950 and Japan's Emergence as a Global Power,* his most recent publication is *East Asia and the United States: An Encyclopedia of Relations Since 1784.* Matray also is international columnist for the *Donga libo* in South Korea.